BECOMING A
PHYSICIAN

BECOMING A PHYSICIAN

A Practical and Creative Guide to Planning a Career in Medicine

Jennifer Danek

Marita Danek

John Wiley & Sons, Inc.

New York · Chichester · Brisbane · Toronto · Singapore · Weinheim

Published by John Wiley & Sons, Inc.

Library of Congress Cataloging-in-Publication Data

Danek, Jennifer
    Becoming a Physician : A Practical and Creative Guide to Planning a
    Career in Medicine / Jennifer Danek, Marita Danek
        p.   cm.
    ISBN 0-471-12166-5 (paper : alk. paper)
    1. Medical colleges--Admission.   2. Medicine--Vocational guidance.
    I. Danek, Marita   II. Title.
    R838.4.M37   1997
    610.69--dc20   96-25092
                                                  CIP

Printed in the United States of America

10 9 8 7 6 5 4 3 2 1

*To Mom, Dad, Jody, and Geoff, who are
my closest friends. If I could only give to
the world what you have given me.*

Jennifer

*To Joe, whose positive spirit and energy
have been the driving force behind
what we do.*

Marita

PREFACE

Jennifer Danek

We began writing this book when I was in my senior year of college. I was applying to medical school at the time, oscillating between feelings of excitement about what my future in medicine would hold and feelings of utter frustration with the process of preparing for, and being accepted to, medical school.

When I started out as a pre-medical student at a small university in Virginia, my plan was well laid out: the only choice I had to make was whether to major in biology or chemistry. My objectives were clear: get good grades, do research, join some student organizations, and develop good relationships with professors. It wasn't until I took a class outside of the sciences that my exposure to the world of academics—and the possibilities that come with it—broadened. I remember the professor of that class being discouraged when he found out I was pre-med. One day he remarked that being a pre-med was "a waste of a mind." At the time, I was baffled by this comment; only later did I begin to understand why he held such an impression about pre-medical education.

Pre-medical education tends to polarize students into two camps— the prototypical pre-meds who eschew anything not directly related to the single-minded pursuit of getting into medical school, and those who eventually flee the pre-med curriculum and dismiss the possibility of becoming a doctor for fear of being too narrowly bound, or because of misinformed ideas about the profession. As a result, many students, despite an interest in medicine, never seriously consider pursuing it. Other students, despite the capability to become physicians, are weeded out of science courses in the first semester of their freshman year and never return. Those who do continue on this road face an expensive and often wearying struggle.

Over the years, I confronted many of these dilemmas of pre-medical education on a personal level. After failing my first P-chem exam, I had to admit that for me quantum mechanics was not a passion. Like many other pre-medical students, I had early made the decision to study chemistry based on what I thought would be best for medical school and without knowing that I had other options. But could I change my major after three years? What would medical schools think of this?

Each of us needs something different in the pre-medical years. If someone had told me this years earlier, I might have taken a deeper look at what I wanted out of my education before making hasty decisions. After I left that chemistry exam, I realized what should have been evident from the start—education shouldn't be a painstaking struggle. It should be a process that affirms the individual, that is both challenging and enjoyable, and that allows each of us to learn in our own way.

The last half of my college years were spent in two different worlds. I decided to change my major to Third World studies and engage in activities that were meaningful to me regardless of whether they were "relevant" to medicine or to medical school admission. I was working with student co-ops, attending seminars on educational reform, and organizing on women's issues. At the same time, I continued with the demands of my pre-medical preparation. I would stay up all night on chocolate-covered espresso beans studying for the morning physics quiz or trudge off at the end of the day to my MCAT review class.

When confronted with the application process and looking realistically at my future in medicine, I had to think not only about how I was going to make it but about who else would make it with me. A series of questions arose: Who decides to pursue a career in medicine? How will college students prepare to be physicians? Who will be favored in the application process? And, ultimately, what will the physician of tomorrow look like?

There is no doubt in my mind that we need to rethink the process of becoming a physician at every step along the way. Changes are needed by everyone—by medical school admission committees, professors, and students. This book is directed to one group—the students—and those issues that concern them, particularly the decision to become a physician, pre-medical education, and the application process.

The objective of this book is not to recruit a certain type of person but rather to encourage all people with an interest in medicine to consider it as a realistic possibility. We believe that you should make this decision based on real information about yourself, the steps needed to become a physician, and knowledge about the practice of medicine. For those who have decided, we hope to serve as guides — informed friends — who will help you to manage the demands of the pre-medical years and to make it into medical school.

I hope that this book will suggest a more humane way to become a physician. Rather than establish specific paths to a career in medicine, we give you some of the tools you will need to scout your way. While at points we say "do this" or "you should," we do not intend the book to be just another how-to guide. Inevitably, people will scan the book with this expectation, looking for ready-made designs and easy solutions. Instead, what we offer is complete and accurate information in areas about which readers may be misinformed; a broad perspective on the undergraduate years; and support and advice to keep you going when the way becomes obscure.

When we refer to pre-med — the student and the education — we mean it in the broadest sense. Pre-medical preparation does not simply involve preparation in the sciences; it is everything you learn about yourself and the world that prepares you for medical school and to be a doctor.

The process of becoming a physician begins the day you decide to explore this career. The more actively you engage in this process, we believe, the better physician you will be.

PREFACE

Marita Danek

I've always been intrigued by how people choose careers. A career pretty much defines how we use our waking hours, how we live our lives, and whom we spend our time with. When I was about ten years old, it seemed like every adult I met said, "What are you going to be when you grow up?" This question tormented me—and that was back in the days when women had limited choices. How the heck did I know?

Eventually, I resolved that decision by becoming a counselor and then a counselor educator. My thinking was, If this was so hard for me, it must be hard for others. Maybe I can help.

Over the years, counselors' roles have changed. Now counselors spend less time helping young people with developmental issues such as career choice and more time dealing with dysfunction—family issues, violence, drugs, and abuse. Regrettably, this emphasis is often necessary in our society. But while we counselors are busy responding to crises, we've neglected career programs and developmental services in our educational institutions.

Most young people I meet today—even those well into their twenties—are struggling with career choice. They are grappling with the same questions as I did but with more choices, fewer barriers, and greater economic uncertainty. It's the same struggle on different terrain. Society and the workplace have changed, but the basic question remains: How can one earn a living in a meaningful way?

Jennifer—my daughter and coauthor—was one of the fortunate ones. She decided to become a doctor at a very young age. I never thought she'd stick with that choice. She had a variety of interests, mostly social, and she wasn't the type of kid who went off to her room to play with her chemistry set. In fact, for someone who knew what she wanted, Jennifer went about the business of becoming a physician in a very atypical way.

We decided to write this book when Jennifer was interviewing for medical school. She came home on winter break with tales of her interviews and all of a sudden the immensity of the decisions still to be made hit us both. She had pretty well sailed through (or around) all barriers so far but had still gotten bogged down in the logistics of secondary applications, interviewing, and choosing a medical school.

We believed there was a book in her experiences—a book that would not only describe the nuts and bolts of getting into medical school but also address the human issues: Is medicine right for me? Do I have what it takes to prepare for the field? How can I become a physician without sacrificing the other things in life that I love?

I visited Jennifer last year in San Francisco to interview some of the medical students you meet on these pages. One day we took a walk (I walked, she ran) in Golden Gate Park. We started out on roads and paths where joggers and walkers were plentiful, but quickly Jennifer turned off into a little footpath with ferns and wildflowers and streams along its way. We followed this path for a while, crisscrossed the joggers' path, followed that for a while, then crashed into another path that twisted down a ravine and veered close to a waterfall before it led back to the main road. I couldn't help thinking how different our experience had been from those of the joggers a few yards away running a straight path on concrete. All of us would go home saying, "I ran in Golden Gate Park this morning," but those words would not capture the diversity of our experiences.

Just as there's no one way to run in Golden Gate Park, there's no one way to become a physician. This book allows you to hop off the well-traveled but predictable path to becoming a physician and to explore the byways of undergraduate education and other experiences during your pre-medical years. As long as you know where these paths are and hop back onto the main road from time to time, you'll be fine.

This book should help you make a major life decision and make your journey to your goal more meaningful and enjoyable.

ACKNOWLEDGMENTS

We are indebted to all those who provided their ideas, gentle nudging, and tolerance, and without whom this book would have remained just another dream. The first person to thank is our editor PJ Dempsey, who decided to take a chance on our idea for this book. Since that time she has always known what we needed when we needed it. Thank you for your honesty, your patience, and your bottomless support.

We also wish to convey our appreciation to the rest of the staff at John Wiley & Sons—to Chris Jackson, Elaine O'Neal, Joanne Palmer, John Simko, and many others behind the scenes, including our copyeditor, Alice Cheyer.

The true spirit of this book belongs to the people over the years who have shared their experiences and impressions about the process of becoming a physician. In particular, we are deeply grateful to the eight medical students and recent graduates who offered their stories as an example of what it means to be a human being struggling to find and create meaningful work. They are Ali Atri, Anita Demas, Elena Hammond, Ivan Hayward, Huong Hyunh, Lloyd Johnson, James Justice, and Facika Tafara.

We also want to thank Drs. José Rodríguez and Robert Shapiro for their advice and encouragement over the years. A special thanks to Dr. Peter Muennig, who cowrote Chapter 10, Choosing a Medical School, and contributed valuable insights and writing to Chapter 13, Making the Transition to Medical School.

Much appreciation goes to those people who provided feedback on the manuscript in its various stages of development. This includes faculty and friends at the University of California School of Medicine, San Francisco, particularly Dr. Anthony Drake and Dr. Emilie Osbourne. A super thanks to Stuart Murray for allowing us to e-mail chapters across the ocean for his comments, to Ed Allred for his help with the cover, and to Barb Koziarz for her suggestions and support. We also appreciate the careful research assistance of Jackie Duba during the early stages of our writing.

An enormous debt is owed to Chris Martin—our on-call writer, editor, production manager, and devoted friend.

And finally, we want to recognize the support and love of everyone in our family—Joe, Jody, and Geoffrey—for sharing our excitement, for believing in us, and for coping with our craziness as we put this together.

CONTENTS

PART ONE

MEDICINE TODAY: A CALLING OR A CAREER CHOICE?

1

THE CHALLENGE
OF CHOOSING

I n earlier times, a person was *called* to be a healer. In aboriginal
societies, the healing shaman was chosen as a young child. This
person usually had spiritual visions or had survived life-threatening
illness early in life. Indigenous doctors, for instance, the *curanderos* in
South America, passed on their art to those in the community who
possessed special abilities, who could harness the healing powers of
nature and the gods.

Most physicians today still consider medicine to be a calling. Yet,
in modern societies, medicine is also a career choice. You are not born
a healer, nor are you selected at a young age to be a physician. You
decide to become a physician. Various forces influence your choice:
your parents, the school courses you like and are good at, early role
models, life experiences, and many others. As you begin to consider
medicine as a career, you need to sort through these influences to
make the decision that's best for you.

IS MEDICINE RIGHT FOR YOU?

In the United States today you have the luxury of choosing from
more than 22,000 careers. How do you begin to narrow down this vast
field and choose the career—and the life—that is best for you?

In this book, we invite you to think about what it means to become
a physician and how this career choice will affect the way you will live
your life. Once you are comfortable with your decision, you will be
able to commit yourself to whatever it takes to get into and through
medical school and to navigate other hurdles along the way.

You begin the process of choosing a career as a physician by understanding yourself: your likes and dislikes, what you consider satisfying or tedious, exciting or stressful. You also must appreciate what a physician's work involves and what preparation is required to enter the profession. If most of what you enjoy can be found in medicine, if you know you have it in you to do this work, and you are willing to invest many years to train for the profession, then you may indeed have a calling to medicine.

Don't Be Discouraged by Physician Stereotypes

You may have preconceived ideas of what doctors are like: their appearance, the way they act, or how they live. You may wonder if you fit the image of a doctor. Do you have that strong exterior, the gentle touch, the confident voice? Can you picture yourself cleaning up after sixteen hours of surgery and teeing off at the local country club?

Forget all that. Physicians do not fit any one stereotype. They have different backgrounds, different personalities, and may be attracted to medicine for different reasons. Some individuals decide at an early age to become a doctor; others turn to medicine later in adulthood. Some are academically gifted; others are hard workers who can achieve through persistence. Some come from comfortable backgrounds, others from environments torn by family strife, poverty, and even war.

Physicians Come from Different Backgrounds

As the population of the United States becomes heterogeneous, its diversity is reflected in the student population of U.S. medical schools. Consider some current medical students and recent graduates who exemplify this diversity:

Ali, whose father was imprisoned during the Iranian Revolution, escaped with his family to England and then to the United States. He entered a state university at age sixteen and went straight through to earn a Ph.D. degree in biomathematics before entering medical school.

Anita grew up in a suburb of Washington, D.C., and graduated with a straight A average in math from an Ivy League college. A successful investment banker for two years, she became disillusioned with the sexism and sexual harassment she experienced in her firm. Volunteer work in a hospital convinced her that medicine would be a more satisfying career for her.

Elena had an early interest in becoming a doctor but was later torn between medicine and literature. She thought about becoming an English professor but felt it was "too removed from the real world." For her, becoming a physician means giving back to society all that it has given her.

Facika felt a subtle family pressure to become a physician. As a pre-med student at an Ivy League school, she was less competitive and less interested in science than her peers. Burned out by the time she graduated from college, she worked for two years as a health care administrator in Africa before deciding that hands-on health care was where she could make a contribution.

Huong is the daughter of a Vietnamese mother and an American father she never knew. When Huong was sixteen, Huong and her younger brother came to the United States and lived with a foster family. She learned English, graduated from college, and entered medical school seven years later, at age twenty-three.

Ivan, who knew he wanted to do something other than take over his father's TV repair shop when he grew up, was a self-described "nerd" in high school and college, and worked hard to escape his family's financial worries. Looking back, he knows he did everything "right" to get into medical school but wonders if he really knew what he was getting himself into and whether he sacrificed too much.

James, an athlete and a scholar, sometimes lowered his standards to fit in with his peers. In college, he learned to set goals and worked to reach them. Along the way, his mother, a single parent, together with a college counselor recognized his potential and helped him reach his goals.

Lloyd had a satisfying and productive career as a Ph.D.-level physicist before choosing medicine as a second career. He returned to college to complete his undergraduate prerequisites, volunteered in a hospital, did well on the MCATs and his interviews . . . and still did not get into medical school. One year later, he reapplied to more schools and became a forty-nine-year-old first-year medical student.

Each of these students did it in a unique way. And we encourage you to do the same—to affirm who you are in the process of becoming a physician rather than conforming to a traditional stereotype.

Throughout this book, you will hear from these students—about when they decided to become doctors and why, the difficulties they encountered, and how they surmounted them.

IT TAKES TIME TO KNOW WHAT YOU WANT OUT OF LIFE

A rare few are fortunate to know from an early age what they want to do in life; they seem to fall effortlessly into the right career. Elena was attracted early to medicine:

> I was fascinated by my little brother's cuts and bruises and always wanted to bandage him up. My best friend suggested we both grow up and become nurses and marry twin brothers who were doctors. I remember saying no, we should become doctors and marry twin brothers who were nurses.

Many of us, however, need time to determine what we want to do. The decision to become a doctor may not be made until later in life.

Facika, for example, worked four years in international development as an administrator before returning to her original plan to become a physician:

> My work in Africa was very health-related. But I realized I was not cut out to be an administrator. Hands-on work would be more exciting. So I went down the list of other things I could do and came back to medicine.

Anita, on the other hand, originally rejected the idea of medicine:

> My mother mentioned something to me about becoming a doctor when I was four, and I thought, "I'm never going to be a doctor," just because she mentioned it. So I majored in math and became an investment banker. At first it was exciting, but slowly I became disillusioned. Then I started volunteering in the Emergency Room at a local hospital and loved it. It had meaning.

BEGIN BY UNDERSTANDING YOURSELF

For most people, choosing a career is a process that involves time, considerable thought, and just plain hard work. One of the most difficult aspects of this process is understanding oneself—the internal mechanisms that guide one's thoughts and actions. Occasionally we catch glimpses, but rarely do we understand how the pieces come together as a whole.

You begin by examining key aspects of your personality that you can discern: what you enjoy (your interests), what you find meaningful (your values), and what you are good at (your abilities and achievements).

What Do You Enjoy?

Ideally, you should not have to force yourself to be interested in what you do, but rather you should make a life—and a career—out of what interests you.

Your interests are constantly evolving. That's why it is important to identify the interests that have persisted over your lifetime and the new ones that emerge. Do you enjoy dealing with people? Have you been fascinated by the human body since you were a child? Do you still enjoy science?

According to John Holland, a well-known career theorist, if you know what your interests are, you can determine what type of work environment and responsibilities would suit you best. Holland groups individuals into six categories based on their interests: Realistic, Investigative, Artistic, Social, Enterprising, and Conventional. Physicians and individuals in health-related careers usually have an Investigative-Social-Artistic (ISA) pattern of interests.

Let's dissect this ISA pattern and examine each of these interest categories in plain language. First, to enjoy medicine, you should be investigative (I) or intellectually inquisitive. Medical professionals are typically perceptive individuals who are curious about the world around them and have a desire to find answers. The next category, social (S) interests, simply means that you like working with people and are able to connect with others' experiences and feelings. Last, you should have artistic (A) interests. Artistic individuals have a unique perspective on the world and relish finding novel solutions to situations and problems as they arise. For more information about Holland's theory of vocational personalities and work environments, see Appendix A.

On the one hand, Holland's categories are generalizations and can disguise important differences among individuals. On the other hand, if you don't see yourself in any of these descriptions, or your interest profile is very different from ISA, you should ask, Is the desire to become a doctor coming from me, or am I responding to goals someone else has set for me?

What Gives Your Life Meaning?

The joy that you take in certain activities and the ways you choose to spend your time reflect more than your interests. They also speak of your values.

People often talk about finding their "life's work." The difference between a job and a life's work is *meaning*. Your work has greater meaning when it is in tune with your values.

Elena saw medicine as a way to contribute:

> My parents instilled in me the belief that you have to be socially responsible and that you should be out there in the community helping people, doing real things, communicating some of your knowledge to others. Medicine was appealing to me because it was psychologically grounded in terms of being real and palpable.

Ali came to medicine after earning his degree in biomathematics:

> I don't want to be in this world solely to respirate—to take in glucose and air and put out carbon dioxide and water. I want to have some kind of impact. My impact doesn't have to be on a global level—like eradicating disease or poverty. Instead, I want to say, "I helped Mrs. Smith today." And if I were off doing math, that wouldn't happen.

Using the questions in the box, you are invited to explore your values to determine if they are integral to medicine and the work of a physician.

Your Values and Medicine

How Suited Are You to a Physician's Work?

Is it a priority for you to contribute to the well-being of others?

Can you see yourself taking responsibility for decisions that affect another person's life?

Do you find it rewarding to help other people?

Are you willing to work irregular hours, and possibly sacrifice your evenings and weekends for your work?

Can you tolerate uncertainty?

Do you find joy in the ordinary aspects of people's lives?

Can you work in an environment that is often hectic and stressful?

Are you able to remain humble in a position that is often characterized by prestige and recognition?

Are you motivated to learn independently and stay up-to-date with current medical advances?

There are no right or wrong answers to these questions. However, they are important to consider, for the answers will help you determine the degree to which your values would be realized by a career in medicine.

It is possible that this exercise will reveal that you are not well suited to life as a physician, despite interests that seem compatible with medicine. You may enjoy working with people but not feel comfortable with the amount of personal responsibility for patients' well-being that you would have to take on. Or you might value a career that is more relaxed, a career that you could leave behind when you leave the office. If this is the case, you may want to investigate other careers, perhaps in one of the allied health professions.

What Are Your Abilities and Achievements?

While your interests and values may nudge you in the direction of a particular career, your abilities will determine your success in that field. Scholastic ability, in particular, influences the likelihood of succeeding in the undergraduate years and in the academic part of medical school. Another essential ability for physicians is the capacity to connect with another human being—to be able to put yourself in another's place and empathize with what that person is experiencing.

Your abilities tend to be innate aspects of who you are—a reflection of your potential. Achievement is how well you use your potential to achieve your goals—a measure of personal effort. We all know people with "so much potential," who score high on all the standardized tests but who still cannot get it together to achieve, or those with incredible social abilities who don't put them to good use. Similarly, we often see people whose innate abilities do not place them at the very top of their class but who still achieve extremely well because of their persistence, hard work, and dedication. In the end, it's achieving your potential—academically and personally—that matters.

Ivan recalls when he started to achieve:

> It was around that jump to ninth grade that I started saying, "Wait a minute—if I don't get my act together and start applying myself a bit, I'm not going to go anywhere—I'm just going to be working in my father's TV shop for the rest of my life." So I started working harder.

Do you have the academic ability and stamina to become a doctor? Are you able to relate to people from a variety of backgrounds as well as to your peers, contribute to a group, and develop intimacy with other human beings? Have you been able to use your talents and abilities to achieve? If the answers to these questions are yes, you may be on your way to a career in medicine.

Huong and James began to consider medicine as an option after academic successes. Huong describes her early college years:

> At first, it would take me seven hours to read a chapter. When I passed my first biology class with an A, I felt, like, "I can do it." After that, I said to myself, "You can do well in any class if you put effort to it."

James remembers his first visit to a pre-medical advisor:

> It was cool that my college had a black counselor. I had just gotten an A in O-Chem [Organic Chemistry] and he said,

"Damn, James, as long as I've been here. I've never known a brother to get an A in O-Chem. You've really got something going here and you should take full advantage of it." I was also starting to handle myself better socially. So I started thinking maybe I could try to work in the life sciences.

Once Huong and James began to achieve, they gained a sense of competence and self-confidence. Perhaps it was recognizing these achievements that motivated them to strive for more successes.

Can You Keep Up the Effort to Reach Your Goal?

In order to achieve your goals, you will need to push past many hurdles. This is where your inner drive, or motivation, is important. James remembers when he wanted to quit Little League: "My mother told me never take myself out, let someone else take me out first. Don't be a quitter." Anita and Lloyd decided to return to school in order to complete the undergraduate requirements necessary to get into medical school. Elena struggled with painful medical problems. Huong persisted with her studies despite the fact that English was not her native language. In looking back at her life in Vietnam, she acknowledges,

> I could have stayed in Vietnam. Become a parent, become a housewife, become a prostitute. Whatever. Just to get an education, to make the best of myself, to think that someday I may be useful to somebody—that was the thing that kept me going.

If you have had a history of solid achievements and can tackle a task with high energy, you know you are capable of achieving what you set out to do. However, if staying the course is difficult for you— if you tend to give up or become discouraged easily—you should think carefully about undertaking a career that requires many years of study and dedication. It comes down to how much you want to become a physician and whether you are willing to make sacrifices— some minor, some great—to reach your goal.

ENVISION YOUR FUTURE
AS A PHYSICIAN

So far we have encouraged you to look inward, to get a sense of who you are as a person. Now you need to connect who you are with what you will do as a physician. Take a few minutes to visualize the life of a physician by considering the questions in the box.

Visualizing Your Future as a Physician

Imagine that you have just begun your first year of practicing medicine. Close your eyes and visualize what your life is like.

Your Work

What kind of medical practice do you have?

How do you spend most of your time at work?

How do you feel when you arrive in your office or at the hospital in the morning?

How do you feel when you leave at night?

Who are your colleagues, and how do you feel about them?

What special satisfactions do you have in your day?

What frustrations do you have, and how do you cope with them?

In looking back, what aspects of your training or specialty choice would you change?

Your Life

Where do you live—small town, city, rural area, or suburb?

What is your neighborhood like? What do you see when you look out your front window?

Who lives with you, and how do you spend your time together?

Who are your friends, and what do you do with them?

How do you spend your leisure time?

How would you rate your overall satisfaction with your life?

What would you change about your life if you could?

Ask yourself if the images that come to mind as you answer these questions are realistic and attainable. If you are pulling a blank to these questions, you may not know enough about the practice of medicine yet to effectively consider your life and work as a doctor.

LEARN ABOUT THE PRACTICE OF MEDICINE

Before you commit so much time, effort, and expense to becoming a physician, you should investigate every aspect of a physician's work. To get more information, you might want to interview physicians from different specialties, volunteer in a medical setting, or spend some time with medical students finding out about their lives. Career counseling and testing may also be valuable (see Appendix B).

As you gather more information about the practice of medicine, you should periodically return to the previous exercise and envision yourself as a doctor. When it starts to feel right—once you are confident that you have both the qualities of a physician and a good understanding of the field—this may be when you have truly decided.

IT'S DOING WHAT YOU LOVE THAT MATTERS

Anita recalls the moment she decided to leave investment banking for medicine:

> It was at a 6:00 A.M. breakfast meeting with one of the partners in my firm. We're on the thirtieth floor sitting around a walnut table eating our fruit cups. This partner was reminiscing about the days when he was an analyst and how much he loved banking. He said, "I love it so much, I think it's a joke that they even pay me. I would do it for free." (He was making $5 million a year.) That was my epiphany. I said to myself, "I would never do this for free. It's so obvious, why did it take me twenty-three years to figure it out? A career is something you'd do for free. If you can figure that out, you've won the game."

The amount of time and effort involved and how much money you'll earn are secondary considerations compared to the joy of doing what you love. You've won the game, as Anita realized, if you can find pleasure in the intrinsic aspects of a physician's work—the challenge of diagnosis, the interaction with patients, or the sense that somehow you have alleviated pain and suffering.

PLAN YOUR COURSE OF ACTION

Once you decide to become a physician, you will need to commit yourself to a course of action. You do not have to take the safe and sure route along with four thousand other pre-med students at your university. What you do need to think about is, What is the best way for *me* to get there.

James began planning early in college:

> I took a goal-setting course. It was one of the best things I could have done. They emphasized setting a realistic long-term goal that you can internalize and intermediate goals you can achieve. I was persistent and planned strategies to reach my goals. When I decided I was going to medical school, I *knew* I was going to medical school.

Lloyd similarly planned to overcome obstacles:

> Once I knew what I wanted to do, in fact needed to do, for the rest of my life, there was no quitting. I went back and completed undergraduate science requirements to make my application stronger. Then I volunteered at a hospital and worked in a lab in that year between my first and second medical school applications.

EVALUATE WHERE YOU ARE GOING AND WHY

Your decision to become a physician will need to be evaluated over time. As demonstrated by Anita's decision to leave investment banking, a career that may seem right at age eighteen or even twenty-five may no longer hold the same appeal a few years later. It makes sense to periodically take stock of how you've changed as a person and where you are going in life.

Reevaluating your commitment to medicine once you start on the path is difficult. If you decided to become a physician years ago and never looked at alternatives, you may fear that your present plans would not stand up to thoughtful scrutiny. Even those who appear to follow a straight path from early decision to medical school are not always as sure as they appear.

Jennifer announced at age six that she would be a doctor. As she grew up, she never wavered in her decision. Then, in the summer before medical school, she went through a difficult period of self-analysis. She worried that after all her work, planning, and hopes, medicine might not be what she wanted after all. She decided to leave for medical school with her mind still open and her decision pending.

As you gain a deeper knowledge of yourself and learn more about medicine, you may reaffirm that medicine is your life's work. Then again, maybe you'll decide to open the proverbial worm farm in Maine. Whatever—it will be your choice.

2

UNDERSTANDING THE PRACTICE OF MEDICINE

Popular images of doctors are often based on myth and misconception. For a long time, our images of physicians were romanticized: the tireless healer kneeling at the bedside of a dying patient, or a country doctor trudging through snow-covered woods to deliver a baby. To these were added dramatic images of the brilliant diagnostician making snap decisions, or the rugged and confident surgeon saving lives. Most recently, a less flattering image of doctors has emerged as individuals who care less about patients than about the financial rewards and status of an elite profession.

Each of you has your own impressions of doctors and medicine — perhaps from your encounters with the health care system, from reading, or from watching television shows like *ER*. These images are snapshots that may capture a certain moment, a particular setting or time, but that reveal little about the whole spectrum of medical practice.

Ivan, now a radiologist in a group practice, admits that he had only a vague understanding of his future life as a physician:

> If you do well in school, you start to think of certain professions. My girlfriend's father was a pediatrician — very erudite and impressive. But as far as knowing what I was getting into and what it meant to be a doctor, I had no idea. I was in the third year of college before I spent any time in a hospital.

This lack of knowledge poses a problem for those considering medicine as a career. How can you decide to enter a career when you don't know what a physician does? How can you know what the practice of medicine will be like in the future? Before you commit to this field, you will need answers to these questions.

ALLOPATHIC AND OSTEOPATHIC MEDICINE: SOME DISTINCTIONS

The majority of physicians are trained as Doctors of Medicine (M.D.s); others attend osteopathic medical schools and are trained as Doctors of Osteopathy (D.O.s). Medical school graduates in both areas are concerned with the diagnosis, treatment, and prevention of disease or injury and are fully trained and licensed to prescribe medication and perform surgery.

Minor differences separate the two fields. Allopathic physicians (M.D.s) rely heavily on traditional treatment modalities, including pharmacological treatment and surgery. Osteopathic physicians have a holistic, preventive approach, that emphasizes the musculoskeletal system and the communication and regulatory channels of the body. While osteopathic physicians use the methods of allopathy in practice, they are also trained in osteopathic manipulation and other techniques designed to restore appropriate body structure and circulation and to stimulate the body's own defense mechanisms against disease. Unlike M.D.s, most D.O.s are in primary care and tend to practice in smaller communities.

PREPARING TO BECOME A PHYSICIAN

Becoming a physician requires a long and intensive period of preparation. It begins in the undergraduate years of college. During this time, you will gain the academic background that is necessary to tackle the Medical College Admissions Test (MCAT) and to succeed in medical school. Most medical schools, both allopathic and osteopathic, have specific admissions requirements, particularly in the sciences, and require at least three years of undergraduate schooling.

Four years of medical school and the attainment of the M.D. degree are followed by three to four years—but it could be as many as seven—of residency (specialty training). Osteopathic physicians must enter a year of general internship before deciding on specialty training. All medical students must pass the National Medical Board Exam, Part 1 (usually after the second year of medical school) and Part 2 (in the fourth year) to graduate from medical school. During your residency, you will also be required to take various licensing and certification exams before you can practice independently. Many specialties require continuing education credits to stay licensed.

Preparing to become a physician can be expensive. According to the Association of American Medical Colleges (AAMC), the average tuition and fees for the first year of medical school in 1995–1996 ranged from a low of $9,447 (for an in-state resident at a state medical school) to a high of $24,131 (for students attending a private medical school). Students who fund their medical education even partly through loans can easily accrue large debts that must be repaid out of future income.

A LOOK INTO THE FUTURE OF MEDICINE

The practice of medicine ten years from now may be very different from what it is today. Let's take a look at some of the trends in medicine.

Patients Are Changing

Hippocrates is reported to have said, "I would rather know what sort of person has a disease than what sort of disease a person has." The next time you pass a bus stop or go to the grocery store, look around. Most of the people you see will be patients at some time in their lives. As a physician, you need to know more than the medical history of these people who are your patients: you will need to understand the context of your patients' lives.

Your patients will come from different cultural, ethnic, and economic backgrounds—all factors that influence their health. Currently, older African Americans have more diabetes, hypertension, and glaucoma than other groups. Whites are more likely to have acute conditions, such as respiratory infections. Latinos have an increased risk for lung cancer and tuberculosis.

In the future, more of your patients will be older. Many of these individuals will have chronic illness or diseases associated with aging, such as arthritis, Alzheimer's disease, and Parkinson's disease. These people will not be "cured" as much as educated to live with their disease and manage their limitations. In addition, demand for end-of-life medical services will increase.

Patients also have become sophisticated consumers of what is now the largest enterprise in the United States—our health services industry. They will demand more openness and equality in their interactions with you. They may challenge you, get second and third opinions, or shop around for another physician if they think you're not up to speed.

Ivan was not prepared for what he encountered in his two years of clinical rotation:

> I dealt with many patients who were very demanding, and it was not the kind of doctor-patient thing you read about in Steinbeck novels, where you were helping people and they were grateful. They'd say, "I read about something, and I want to get it done on me, and why aren't you doing it, doctor?" Then, too, I was seeing people treated who couldn't be helped—resectioning their colon, taking out a portion of their liver, giving them chemotherapy and radiation and watching their hair fall out and finally they were gone and you'd say, "Well, we tried everything we could."

Health Problems Are Changing

Diseases that killed in the past have been nearly eradicated: whooping cough, polio, smallpox, and many others. Antibiotics have appreciably reduced the mortality rate from ruptured appendixes, postpartum infections, pneumonia, and bacterial infections.

And yet, other problems have surfaced. Currently, we are seeing a resurgence of tuberculosis, ear infections, and infectious diseases, largely because of bacterial resistance to antibiotics. AIDS has become the leading cause of death in certain populations. Many other diseases are not well understood or easily treated, such as multiple sclerosis or chronic fatigue syndrome.

Increasing societal ills are responsible for a large share of health problems. In the future, physicians will most likely see more child, elder, and spousal abuse, drug and alcohol problems, and sexually transmitted diseases. You will have patients with diseases related to poverty, unemployment, homelessness, overcrowding, or inadequate nutrition. Violence, particularly gun injuries, adds billions each year to health costs.

Many of our health problems are lifestyle- or work-related. People who work with heavy machinery, for instance, may be at risk for noise-induced hearing loss (NIHL). More than 400,000 deaths in the United States yearly are associated with cigarette smoking. In the future, physicians will need to take a greater role in preventing illness by counseling patients about lifestyle changes and occupational hazards.

Many people with health complaints have no identifiable physical problems. Often, their symptoms are due to anxiety, depression, or other emotional problems. These people do not need the latest technological advances; instead they need information, psychological counseling, or as one medical student noted, "simply someone to talk to."

Practice Is Changing

You may know older physicians who are angry or disillusioned about the way the practice of medicine has changed over the past few decades. What's all the fuss about? Certainly, technology and treatment have changed, but most physicians can deal with that. For most, changes in "the system" are what's burdensome—more hassles with reporting, more interference by insurance companies, more concerns over malpractice litigation.

In the next decade, the practice of medicine will undergo even more changes. Pressure to cut costs, to respond to changing patient needs, physician demographics, and initiatives from insurance companies or public programs will all play a role in the reshaping of American medicine.

Here are some issues and projections for your future work as a physician.

PHYSICIAN SUPPLY
The nationwide demand for physicians is estimated to be 205 physicians per 100,000 population. Based on this figure, the American

Medical Association (AMA) predicts that there will be a 5 percent surplus of physicians by the year 2000.

And yet, the distribution of doctors is uneven. Most physicians practice in cities rather than in rural, poorer areas. In some areas of the country, there are as few as 30 physicians per 100,000 population. There are also many more specialists than currently needed, with a shortage of primary care physicians (family medicine, general internal medicine, and general pediatrics).

What does this mean for you? In the next decade, you will need to look realistically at how and where you practice. Competition for employment in specialized areas is expected to increase, with a limited number of residency slots available to medical school graduates in many states. The greatest opportunities will be in the primary care specialties, particularly in rural areas.

Fortunately, most new physicians will not need to worry about unemployment. Lifestyle changes among physicians, such as shorter hours, time out for child rearing, reduced patient loads, and earlier retirement, along with an increase in the number of physicians on salary are expected to lead to a reduced workload—not necessarily a bad thing.

MALPRACTICE REFORM

Medical malpractice concerns have multiplied for physicians and hospitals. Juries are awarding high claims, medical insurance premiums are growing, and physicians are cautious about seeing high-risk patients.

Who controls the quality of services you will provide to your patients? In the past, the physician decided what medical treatment to provide, and how. Today, the government, insurance companies, and the courts monitor health care. Many physicians decry this loss of professional autonomy. The threat, as they see it, is to their professional judgment and the freedom to treat patients as they best see fit.

And yet physicians can make mistakes. They can also be incompetent. The "bureaucratization" of medicine is part of a general trend to increase accountability and maintain professional standards across all sectors of society.

Regrettably, the threat of malpractice in the past few decades has changed the way physicians practice medicine. Physicians order more diagnostic tests, enter narrowly defined specialties so that they are only responsible for problems in their areas of expertise, and limit their practices in order to lower malpractice insurance premiums. The U.S. Congress is currently addressing these issues, and there is a good chance that caps on monetary court awards and other concerns will be resolved by the time you begin to practice medicine.

CONTROLLING COSTS

U.S. medical costs in recent decades have burgeoned because of more physicians, more hospitals, more specialized services—and the excess use of all these.

Who will pay for the medical services you will provide as a physician? At one time, your patient paid you out of pocket. Then medical costs became higher. The increase in the cost of medical care was temporarily resolved with health insurance—individual, employment-based, and eventually government-funded programs like Medicare (for the elderly) and Medicaid (for the poor). While private insurance and government funding for health care increased patients' access to medical services, it also led to increased spending by both patients and physicians because the real costs were being covered by a third party. As a result, the cost of health insurance skyrocketed, and public funding was progressively cut, until many people could not afford private insurance and were no longer covered by government programs.

Today, a growing number of Americans are uninsured or under-insured. Without adequate health insurance, many people do not have access even to basic health care. Thus, there has been a push for health care reform to provide universal coverage to all Americans. The United States is currently the only industrialized nation that does not provide universal health coverage for all its citizens, despite the fact that approximately 12 percent of our gross national product (GNP) goes to health care—one of the highest percentages in industrialized countries.

In the midst of the recent debate over health care reform, more cost-effective ways of providing health care and paying medical costs, such as prepayment systems, have taken hold. Prepayment systems are the hallmark of managed care. In a managed care system, instead of paying for a routine checkup or procedure (a "fee-for-service" arrangement), the patient (or the patient's employer) pays a fixed annual premium to an organization such as a health maintenance organization (HMO), which provides access to a network of physicians. This fee covers standard health services regardless of how often those services are required. Thus, the organization and the physicians who have contracted with it have an incentive to keep down medical expenditures or lose their profit.

Fifty or so years ago, prepayment for health services was considered unethical by the AMA. Today, health care reform is hastening the pace in this direction. Within the next decade, probably half of all Americans will receive medical services from an HMO or similar managed health care network.

On the positive side, managed care organizations emphasize primary care and preventive medicine, reduce unnecessary use of specialized services, and maintain high standards for quality assurance. They offer access to reasonably priced health care for millions of Americans who could otherwise not afford it.

However, managed care has drawbacks for both patients and physicians. Both have complained about a surge in administrative paperwork and red tape. Patients may choose from only a limited number of physicians in a network and aren't always assured of seeing the same physician. For physicians, it means more oversight and less autonomy in making treatment decisions about individual patients. Physicians also may be dropped from a network, in which case they would lose some of their patient population.

Some health policy experts worry that the profit incentive or the fear of being dropped from a network may encourage physicians to cut costs at the expense of patients' health. Although some recent research shows that patient utilization of services is down in HMOs that use a capitation system (fixed fees per patient), one can't infer from these data that physicians in HMOs are skimping on patient care. They may be an indication of what we need—efficient and appropriate use of scarce medical resources.

It boils down to this: whether in managed care networks, private practice, or public community clinics, physicians in the future will need to be increasingly aware of financial restraints when making clinical decisions. You will need to consider cost when deciding which lab tests are needed, whether specialized care is warranted, and even how much time should be spent with patients.

A PHYSICIAN'S WORK: TECHNICAL KNOWLEDGE AND THE HEALING ARTS

As we have said, medicine appeals to individuals with an Investigative-Social-Artistic (ISA) constellation of interests. For a long time, the investigative aspects of medicine—using technical knowledge and skills to solve health problems—have been emphasized above all else.

The medical school admissions process has typically favored students with high levels of academic achievement. Yet the skills that tend to make students academically successful—obsessive study habits, competitive behavior, and a drive to succeed—may not be the only or most important ones they need to succeed as physicians. Especially in future years, as more physicians practice primary care, practitioners will need to be skilled in listening to patients' concerns and taking a comprehensive medical history, developing rapport, and showing sensitivity to the needs of patients and their families.

Today the Association of American Medical Colleges encourages medical schools to choose applicants for their personal qualities, not just academic performance. Employers increasingly emphasize human relations skills along with technical competence. Advertisements for health plans carry the message: "Here, you're not just a number."

Return to the Bedside Manner

Any first-year medical student can tell you how friends and family buttonhole them with symptoms every time they come home. Jennifer was deluged with questions from elderly neighbors about their medical conditions the summer *before* she entered medical school. Why weren't these people telling their stories to their own physicians? Evidently, many people feel that physicians don't have the time—or the interest or ability—to listen and respond to their concerns.

What the public yearns for is a physician with a good bedside manner. As a physician, you should be comfortable dealing with patients' feelings. You need to know how to handle difficult behavior in people who are afraid and sick.

Huong describes an experience in the Emergency Room in her second year of medical school:

> This woman was sixty years old and had been a heroin addict since she was eleven. She had destroyed her body . . . abscesses all over her. She was cursing at the doctors, "You are so stupid, you let these kids learn to be doctors and practice on me, causing me so much pain." I walked out, and when I walked back in, she was still cursing. So I sat next to her and started listening to her, and she stopped cursing and started talking about her four children and her fears and why she does heroin. As a physician, I need to maintain that level of caring as part of my total responsibility. You can drain the abscesses and suture the wounds, but if patients are not healed as a person, they inflict those same wounds again and again until they die.

Sadly, healing the whole person rather than the wound itself has been overshadowed by the technical side of medicine. And yet, advances in medical technology and scientific knowledge actually increase the importance of the doctor-patient relationship and the need for clear communication. Part of your responsibility as a physician will be to demystify complicated medical options so that patients and their families can make informed treatment choices. For example, how do you introduce to parents the idea that their twelve-year-old son who was killed riding his bike an hour ago would be an ideal organ donor? How do you explain to terminally ill patients the latest advances in treatment if none of them offer much hope? How do you clarify to adult children what will happen if they take their aged parent off life support? How do you communicate to heartbroken parents their chances of having another child die of a rare genetic disease? In another time, such scenarios and decisions would have been unimaginable.

Physicians also need interpersonal skills to develop positive relationships at work, create and manage groups of health professionals, resolve conflicts, and consult with experts outside your area of competence. As we move toward managed care, you will need to collaborate more with nonphysician health care providers—physicians' assistants, nurse practitioners, podiatrists, psychologists, chiropractors, and other professionals.

Attributes to Connect to Yourself

We have all heard the expression, "Physician, heal thyself." The nature of the work that you as a doctor will do with patients requires that you be in touch with deep levels of meaning in your own life. You need to understand your own feelings about illness and death before you can empathize with sick and dying people. You must be aware of how your own life experiences, values, and personal beliefs may affect your interaction with patients. As a physician, you must be able to step outside your frame of reference and understand the patient's perspective. As James pointed out,

> Suppose you are in the Emergency Room and you tell a patient you have to give him a sigmoidoscopy, and he's a 250-lb angry man who may be homeless and addicted to crack, who has been waiting in the ER for eight hours ... if you've never had any experience with people who are different from yourself, you're not going to be effective. He is going to say, "You're not doing that to me." That's a real feeling for him. And you've got to be able to understand that and to communicate with him.

The work of a physician can engender extraordinary personal growth and also some degree of stress. It involves frequent confrontation with life-and-death issues, heavy workloads with time constraints, concerns about making a mistake that could result in injury or death, and the need to stay current with medical advances. Today, growing pressure to keep costs down, fear of malpractice litigation, and government regulations contribute even more stress.

Occupational stress can lead to social or psychological problems for physicians, including alcohol abuse, chemical dependence, and domestic violence. Some data suggest that the incidence of substance abuse may be greater for medical students than for the general student population.

To cope with the demands of medical practice, physicians should have or develop an "internal locus of control." This means that you can think independently, rely less on others' opinions of you, and have the capacity for impulse control. You should cultivate high self-esteem—not arrogance (which masks insecurity) but the confidence in yourself that says you are doing the best you can and that you can think and respond competently under pressure.

THE REWARDS
OF MEDICAL PRACTICE

If tomorrow's physician faces more competition, greater regulation of practice, and more uncertainty, what rewards are left to being a doctor?

Certainly, American physicians are and will continue to be relatively well paid. However, financial gain alone cannot provide sufficient reward for years of preparation that are longer than most other occupations require. What's more, the extrinsic rewards of being a physician, such as financial gain, status, and prestige, can and will change over your lifetime.

It is the intrinsic rewards of being a doctor that endure. These are the day-to-day activities of your work that give you a deep sense of fulfillment. It is seeing your patients struggle with life's meanings and finding your own life enriched in the process.

The joy of practicing medicine is illustrated by the attitude of a brand-new resident in ob-gyn (obstetrics and gynecology). When asked why she chose this specialty, with its long, erratic hours and high malpractice premiums, she replied, "Yes, but when you do what you love, you don't think about those things!"

3

SPECIALTIES IN MEDICINE

Hundreds of years ago, when medicine was characterized by practices such as bloodletting, cupping, and purging, a physician managed all areas of medical treatment. However, as our knowledge of the medical sciences grew, and new techniques and remedies were discovered, we began to see signs of specialization in the medical profession: physicians with advanced training in anatomy and physiology, people skilled in setting fractures, birth attendants, or those treating disturbances of the mind.

This trend toward specialization in medicine began with the surgeons in the 1700s and quickened in the second half of the nineteenth century. The discovery of anesthetic agents provided the impetus for new and more advanced surgery. The invention of the cystoscope encouraged specialization in urology. The establishment of special hospitals for children's ailments paved the way for pediatrics.

While specialization originally faced vehement opposition from many within the field, it slowly gained acceptance as a necessary part of progress in the medical profession. In the late 1880s the American Medical Association (AMA) officially recognized more than eighteen different specialty areas in medicine. Today, there are close to one hundred different specialty and subspecialty areas of medicine.

Specialized care makes sense from a patient health perspective. The more patients a doctor sees with similar conditions, the more effective this physician should become. The specialist also can stay more current with developments in one area. Thus, patients with multiple sclerosis, for example, may get more information about the potential benefits and side effects of a new drug from a neurologist who specializes in that area than from a general practitioner.

Specialization, however, has its drawbacks. Instead of seeing one doctor for all problems, it's not uncommon for a person to trek from one specialist to the next—a gynecologist for women's health concerns, a dermatologist for conditions of the skin, a cardiologist to monitor heart problems, and a general internal medicine physician, who takes care of the patient when she has the flu. It's no wonder that many people feel medical care has become fragmented and impersonal.

Too much specialization and the excessive use of high-tech medical services also are blamed for spiraling health care costs. In our modern health care system, specialists and advanced technology abound. At the same time, many people don't have access to a primary care doctor who can take care of basic health needs such as a sore throat or childhood immunizations. This is the downside of over-specialization—too many experts and not enough general doctors.

In the future, the mainstay of medicine will again be the primary care doctor. Still, if we are to continue providing quality specialized services, we will also need some physicians who are trained in areas as diverse as ophthalmology, medical toxicology, or thoracic surgery.

Medical terminology for specialties can be confusing. You shouldn't confuse the term *specialty* with the terms *specialization* or *specialist. Specialty* refers to all fields in medicine that require training and certification after medical school, including both general and specialized care areas. Depending on the degree of specialization, a particular field may be referred to as primary care (least specialized), secondary care, or tertiary care (most specialized).

PRIMARY CARE:
THE GENERALIST SPECIALTIES

Primary care is the point at which a patient enters the health care system. The primary care specialties are sometimes called the generalist specialties and include general family medicine, general internal medicine, and pediatrics. Depending on who is doing the defining, obstetrics and gynecology (ob-gyn) is sometimes also called a primary care specialty.

Primary care physicians diagnose and treat an array of general health problems from the common cold to diabetes. About 80 percent of our health care needs can be met by a primary care physician.

Patients with complicated medical problems or conditions that require advanced technology are referred by the primary care doctor to a specialist in that area.

As our health care system moves toward managed care, primary care doctors are more in demand. The primary care physician is considered to be the gatekeeper of health care, determining when and if a patient needs to be referred to a specialist. Having more primary care doctors is both practical (more people get basic services) and cost-effective, since presumably the primary care doctor will limit referrals to those that are absolutely necessary.

Osteopathic medical schools have long emphasized primary care, with the result that more than 60 percent of D.O.s go into family practice, pediatrics, ob-gyn, and OMT (osteopathic manipulation therapy). The government and the medical community now are encouraging allopathic medical schools to graduate more M.D.s who plan to go into primary care.

General Family Medicine

In a brief time, family practice has grown to be the second largest specialty in the United States. Most of the nation's medical schools now have a family medicine department.

The family physician provides basic medical care for all members of the community—children, adults, and elderly people—mostly in an outpatient setting. A family physician must know the health needs of people of various ages and social groups. He or she treats common medical problems and counsels patients on measures to improve health and prevent disease. Often the family physician will treat a patient over a lifetime.

Since family physicians are concerned with the whole picture of a patient's well-being, they deal with a myriad of medical, social, psychological, and economic issues—with the individual and the community at large. A family doctor must be able to recognize when there is domestic abuse, when a patient is depressed, or how financial limitations may affect care.

General Internal Medicine

Internal medicine is the largest medical specialty in the United States. An internist is an expert in adult disease and the interrelations of every system in the body. In some ways, the work of an internist is similar to and overlaps with that of a family practitioner—both are primary care physicians responsible for adult patient care. The internist, however, tends to treat more patients with complex medical conditions and chronic illnesses, in both outpatient and hospital settings. Internists often serve as consultants to other physicians, particularly with hospitalized patients.

Pediatrics

Pediatricians deal with childhood and adolescent growth and development as well as with the general health concerns of children and young adults. Since a younger population tends to be healthier, the emphasis in pediatrics is on well-child care and providing education to parents. Pediatricians must be able to detect genetic conditions and other diseases of childhood.

General pediatrics is a primary care specialty; however, there are many subspecialty areas in pediatrics, including cardiology, critical care medicine, endocrinology, gastroenterology, hematology-oncology, neonatal-perinatal medicine, nephrology, neurology, pulmonology, and sports medicine.

SECONDARY AND TERTIARY CARE

The next tier of specialization is secondary care. Secondary care focuses on one body system, disease process, or specific population. It includes the medical specialties (e.g., cardiology), the surgical specialties (e.g., general surgery), and the support specialties (e.g., pathology). Secondary care usually requires more advanced technology and services, often provided in a hospital setting.

Further specialization in these fields is known as "tertiary care." For example, a cardiologist may receive further training in cardiac catheterization. A surgeon who deals with the musculoskeletal system is an orthopedic surgeon. A pathologist with a focus in immunology is known as an immunopathologist.

Usually, a specialist sees a patient after the primary care doctor suspects a problem and refers the patient. For example, a family doctor may recognize the warning signs of diabetic retinopathy in a patient with diabetes and refer the patient to a specialist—in this case, an ophthalmologist.

Specialists step in to deal with patients at a specific time, for a specific problem. They serve as consultants to the primary care physician but are not responsible for the total care of the patient. The ophthalmologist may deal with a complication of diabetes, but the long-term management of the disease is left to the primary care physician. Subspecialists serve in a similar way, as consultants to other specialists or to the primary care physician.

The number of specialists and subspecialists is, in most fields, increasing faster than the need for their services. In the past sixty-five years, the number of medical specialists has grown from one-tenth of all U.S. physicians to almost two-thirds.

As a result of this surplus of specialists and the current changes in our health care system, health care experts predict that most specialists will lose some of their patient volume in the future. Specialists who are having particular problems finding positions after residency are mainly in anesthesiology, orthopedic surgery, pathology, plastic surgery, and pulmonary disease. However, some subspecialties in these areas do not have a surplus of doctors, for example, pediatric cardiology. Other areas of specialization, such as physical medicine and rehabilitation, ob-gyn, psychiatry, and urology, have ample employment opportunities.

Since supply and demand in certain specialties can change quickly as the health care system and reimbursement procedures change, you should stay up-to-date on what is happening in any specialty you think you may enter.

Medical Specialties

The medical specialties range from the specialized "referred" fields such as neurology to those whose practitioners focus on a certain population but actually function like primary care doctors, for example, adolescent medicine or geriatric medicine. Some of these fields have their own specialty boards for certification, for instance, allergy and immunology; others are considered subspecialties for purposes of certification, for instance, cardiology is a subspecialty of internal medicine.

ADDICTION MEDICINE/ADOLESCENT MEDICINE

For adolescents, the greatest health threats are behavioral, not biological. Specialists in this field use preventive interventions to reduce the risk of alcohol, tobacco, and other drug usage and also of HIV infection and other sexually transmitted diseases. Counseling skills are particularly important for this type of practice. Adolescent medicine practitioners may have backgrounds in internal medicine or pediatrics.

ALLERGY AND IMMUNOLOGY
This specialty provides medical care for a variety of allergic, asthmatic, and immunologic diseases, such as hay fever, asthma, or hives. In addition, allergists treat gastrointestinal symptoms, inflammation in allergic reactions, migraine, and vascular types of headaches. One subspecialty in this area is clinical and laboratory immunology.

CARDIOLOGY
This subspecialty of internal medicine deals with the functions of the heart, blood vessels, and blood circulation throughout the body. Certification is available in areas such as pediatric cardiology or electrophysiology. Additional training is available in nuclear cardiology and cardiac catheterization.

DERMATOLOGY
Dermatologists specialize in diseases of the skin, hair, nails, and mucous membranes such as acne or fungal infections. Many dermatologists are active in research projects, for instance, the use of sunscreens to reduce skin cancer. One subspecialty in this area is dermatopathology (see Pathology description).

ENDOCRINOLOGY
This subspecialty of internal medicine deals with the endocrine glands—the pituitary, thyroid, parathyroid, adrenals, ovaries, and testes. Endocrinologists may treat diabetes mellitus, growth problems, osteoporosis, reproductive problems, and similar conditions.

GASTROENTEROLOGY
This subspecialty of internal medicine is concerned with digestive diseases of the esophagus, stomach, small and large intestines, gallbladder, liver, and pancreas.

GERIATRIC MEDICINE
This subspecialty emphasizes the maintenance of optimal functioning in old age. The focus in geriatric medicine is on education programs,

individual counseling, and the physiology of aging and common diseases in elderly people. Physicians in geriatric medicine may have a background in family medicine or internal medicine.

HEMATOLOGY

This subspecialty of internal medicine focuses on the treatment of malignant (cancerous) and nonmalignant blood diseases, for example, sickle-cell anemia.

INFECTIOUS DISEASES

This subspecialty of internal medicine focuses on infections caused by viruses, bacteria, fungi, and parasites.

MEDICAL GENETICS

This is a newer, rapidly expanding specialty concerned with the diagnosis, management, and counseling of individuals with genetic or possibly genetic diseases such as Huntington's disease or Alzheimer's disease.

NEPHROLOGY

This subspecialty of internal medicine focuses on the medical (nonsurgical) treatment of people with kidney disease.

NEUROLOGY

Neurologists specialize in the diagnosis and treatment of conditions of the nervous system, including diseases of the brain, spinal cord, the peripheral nerves, and the neuromuscular system, such as multiple sclerosis or myasthenia gravis. Some subspecialties in this area are child neurology and clinical neurophysiology.

OBSTETRICS AND GYNECOLOGY (OB-GYN)

This is a combined specialty that focuses on human sexuality, reproduction, and birth. Obstetricians provide prenatal care and deliver babies; gynecologists provide regular reproductive health care for women. Because these physicians do surgical procedures, this is also considered a surgical subspecialty. Some subspecialties in this area are gynecologic oncology, maternal-fetal medicine, and reproductive endocrinology.

ONCOLOGY
This is a subspecialty of internal medicine devoted to diagnosing, treating, and managing cancers, including leukemia and lymphoma.

PHYSICAL MEDICINE AND REHABILITATION (PHYSIATRY)
This specialty is concerned with the restoration of function in people with neuromusculoskeletal, cardiovascular, pulmonary, and other body system disabilities. Physiatrists evaluate and treat disabilities such as mobility impairments, degenerative arthritis, spinal cord injuries, and similar conditions.

PSYCHIATRY
A psychiatrist specializes in the diagnosis and treatment of people with mental and emotional problems. Psychiatrists provide assessment, individual and group psychotherapy, and psychopharmacologic management. Subspecialties in this area include addiction psychiatry, child and adolescent psychiatry, and forensic psychiatry.

PULMONARY AND CRITICAL CARE MEDICINE
This combined subspecialty of internal medicine deals with respiratory illness and overall health care of patients with serious conditions such as cancer, bacteremia, or aspiration pneumonitis. Critical care medicine can also be a subspecialty of anesthesiology, internal medicine, neurological surgery, obstetrics and gynecology, and pediatrics.

PULMONOLOGY
Pulmonologists are subspecialists in internal medicine who focus on diseases of the respiratory system, including the lungs and bronchial tubes.

RHEUMATOLOGY
Rheumatologists are subspecialists in internal medicine who diagnose and treat inflammatory and musculoskeletal diseases such as rheumatoid arthritis, gout, lupus erythematosus, and various autoimmune diseases.

SPORTS MEDICINE

This is a newer subspecialty focusing on the diagnosis and management of illnesses and injuries related to sports and exercise. Emphasis is on prevention and rehabilitation. Practitioners in this subspecialty may have backgrounds in internal medicine, emergency medicine, family practice, or pediatrics.

Surgical Specialties

Surgeons focus on procedures. Conditions that cannot be managed by a medical specialist might be treated surgically, sometimes under emergency conditions. Hospitals are still the center of most surgeons' work, although outpatient (ambulatory) settings are becoming more popular for many kinds of surgery.

GENERAL SURGERY

General surgeons handle predominantly abdominal surgery (e.g., appendectomies, gallbladder, or ulcer surgery), trauma and wound management, and infection healing. General surgery subspecialties include hand surgery, pediatric surgery, surgical critical care, and vascular surgery.

The specialists in the following areas receive advanced training in a particular type of surgery.

COLON AND RECTAL SURGERY

This specialty deals with medical conditions involving the large intestine and rectum. It requires competence in diagnostic and surgical procedures such as colonoscopy.

NEUROLOGICAL SURGERY

This specialty provides treatment and management of disorders of the brain, skull, spinal cord, peripheral nerves, and related structures. An example of a subspecialty in this area is pediatric neurosurgery.

OPHTHALMOLOGY

This is both a medical and surgical specialty emphasizing diagnosis and treatment of eye diseases and injuries. Training fellowships for ophthalmologists exist in areas such as corneal and external diseases, glaucoma, pediatric ophthalmology, neuro-ophthalmology, ophthalmic pathology, and vitreal-retinal disease.

ORTHOPEDIC SURGERY

Orthopedic surgeons deal with problems of the musculoskeletal system ranging from bone tumors to knee injuries to hip replacements. Examples of subspecialties in this area include adult reconstructive orthopedics, foot and ankle orthopedics, hand surgery, musculoskeletal oncology, orthopedic surgery of the spine, orthopedic trauma, and pediatric orthopedics.

OTOLARYNGOLOGY (HEAD AND NECK SURGERY)

This specialty treats problems of the ear, facial skeleton, nose, and throat that come from trauma, tumors, infections, congenital anomalies, and the aging process. Subspecialties in this area include otology/neurotology and pediatric otolaryngology.

PLASTIC SURGERY

This is a surgical specialty that focuses on the repair and reconstruction of anatomical structures, including cosmetic surgery, the transplantation of tissues, and problems in wound healing and scarring. An example of a subspecialty in this area is hand surgery.

THORACIC SURGERY

This surgical specialty encompasses care of patients with chest conditions, such as coronary artery disease or lung cancer.

UROLOGY

This surgical and medical specialty deals with diseases of the male and female urinary tracts and the male reproductive organs. Subspecialties in this area include male sexual dysfunction and infertility, and pediatric urology.

Support Specialties

The support specialties encompass a number of adjunct specialties critical to individual patient care and societal health.

AEROSPACE MEDICINE
This is a newer subspecialty of preventive medicine that focuses on certification and medical standards for pilots, healthy functioning of operating crews of space vehicles, air medical transport of patients, passenger health and safety, and medical research in space.

ANESTHESIOLOGY
Anesthesiologists create a painless state in the patient and keep track of the patient's vital signs during surgical, obstetrical, and other procedures. Anesthesiologists are expert in pain management, cardiopulmonary resuscitation, respiratory care problems, and the management of patients in special care units. Although most anesthesiologists are hospital-based, some serve in ambulatory centers because of the increased use of outpatient surgery. Examples of subspecialties in this area are anesthesiology critical care and pain management.

EMERGENCY MEDICINE
Emergency medicine ranges from routine primary care to critical care and trauma services. It is the primary source of health care for uninsured patients, victims of violence and natural disasters, and people with sudden cardiac arrest. Subspecialties in this area include medical toxicology, pediatric emergency medicine, and sports medicine.

MEDICAL TOXICOLOGY
This is a subspecialty of preventive medicine that controls environmentally induced diseases or poisoning, for instance, diseases from lead exposure or asbestos inhalation. A medical toxicologist is also an expert in managing the complications of drug overdose.

NUCLEAR MEDICINE
This specialty focuses on the diagnosis and treatment of disease through using imaging techniques with radiopharmaceuticals. Specialists in nuclear medicine may have backgrounds in internal medicine or radiology.

OCCUPATIONAL MEDICINE
Specialists in this subspecialty of preventive medicine are expert in the recognition, treatment, and prevention of illness and injury caused by

workplace and environmental hazards such as noise-induced hearing loss (NIHL), chemical sensitivity, repetitive motion injury, or workplace violence. Physicians in this subspecialty often have a Master of Public Health (M.P.H.) degree.

PATHOLOGY

The pathologist specializes in diseases and disease processes. Pathologists interpret laboratory information, monitor the effects of therapy, perform autopsies, and manage hospital services such as blood banks and diagnostic laboratories. Pathologists usually function as consultants to other physicians and don't work directly with patients. Some subspecialties in this area are blood banking/transfusion medicine, chemical pathology, cytopathology, dermatopathology, forensic pathology, hematology, immunopathology, medical microbiology, neuropathology, and pediatric pathology.

PREVENTIVE MEDICINE AND PUBLIC HEALTH

This specialty emphasizes prevention of disease and injury in communities and defined population groups. The focus is on health, not disease. Activities in this specialty involve formulating health policy; setting up health programs; and teaching about personal and environmental protection and lifestyle choices regarding substance usage, diet, exercise, seat belts, sunscreens, and other preventive efforts. Preventive medicine contributes to the worldwide eradication of certain diseases like guinea worm and polio, and provides consultation on water purification, food protection, and environmental control of diseases such as Lyme disease or Legionnaire's disease. Subspecialties in this area are aerospace medicine, medical toxicology, and occupational medicine.

RADIOLOGY

Radiologists specialize in a variety of diagnostic imaging techniques, including X-ray diagnosis, nuclear radiology, diagnostic ultrasound, magnetic resonance imaging, and other forms of radiant energy. They use radiation for both diagnosis and treatment. Examples of subspecialties in this area include neuroradiology, nuclear radiology, pediatric radiology, and vascular and interventional radiology.

CHOOSING A SPECIALTY

The choice of specialty is the most important decision you will face as a medical student. Chances are you will spend more time in your residency training than you did in medical school. Depending on the field, residency training lasts from three to seven years, or more if you choose to continue with a subspecialty.

Despite the importance of choosing the right specialty, most medical students do not feel well informed about what it would be like to practice in the specialties they are considering. Although medical school rotations provide exposure to core specialties, it is difficult to assess a specialty practice from such limited experience.

Choosing a specialty is more complex than saying, "I'd love to work with children," or "I'm interested in the eye," or "I need a specialty that I can practice in a small city." Many factors enter into the choice of a specialty.

The questions to ask yourself as you think about a medical specialty are similar to those you considered about a medical career. You will need to think through various aspects of the specialty, including the type of patients you want to work with, how challenging you will find the specialty, how much you want to utilize technology and procedures, the competitiveness of the specialty, where you want to live, lifestyle factors, job opportunities, diversity in the field, autonomy in the field, training length and requirements, opportunities for midlife changes in the specialty, and other factors. As with career choice in general, standardized tests and other resources are available to help you make a careful choice of a medical specialty area. The questions in the box bring up some points to consider when deciding on a specialty. For a listing of medical specialty boards and organizations, see Appendix C.

Many of the medical students and young physicians interviewed for this book narrowed down their choice of specialty in the clinical years of medical school. Ali plans to become a neurologist. Ivan did a fellowship in interventional radiology and is now joining a group practice. Elena, Facika, Huong, and Lloyd want to be active in the community as primary care physicians. Anita is attracted to the fast pace of an Emergency Room physician. James is considering a combined academic and surgical career as a liver transplantation specialist.

Things to Consider When Choosing a Specialty

Patients

How important is it for you to be involved in direct patient care?

Do you want to work with a broad cross section of the population or with a specific group of patients?

What kinds of patient health conditions are you interested in working with—patients with chronic conditions or patients with conditions you can cure?

How important is dealing with a diversity of patient problems?

How much do you want to be involved in doctor/patient relationships?

Specialty Characteristics

How important is it for you to use procedures or instrumentation?

How important is it to deal with challenging diagnostic problems?

How important is it to have opportunities to teach or do research?

How much stress can you handle in everyday practice?

How important is it for you to work in a specialty that has high demand for services?

How important is it to be in a cutting-edge specialty where conditions constantly change?

Do you prefer regular hours and few emergencies?

How well do you tolerate ambiguity (e.g., not knowing immediately what is wrong with a patient)?

How well do you deal with controversy or ethical dilemmas?

How important is it for you to have stipend support for your training program?

How important is it to have the option of a midlife change of specialty?

Practice Characteristics

Would you rather get referrals from other physicians or have your patients self-refer?

How important is it for you to practice in an environment with minimum red tape?

(continued)

How important is it to practice on your own terms—do the procedures you like best, set your own hours, and have control of your time?

Would you prefer to work with patients in a hospital setting or with outpatients?

Do you enjoy working with teams of health professionals or on your own?

How much responsibility do you want for supervising or managing others?

How important are community characteristics of where you will practice (e.g., quality of schools, population density, access to public transportation, leisure and cultural activities, proximity to universities)?

4

PRACTICE SETTINGS

Twenty years ago we had a pediatrician who ran his practice out of a little office attached to his home. The office had a staff of three: the doctor, his wife, and a superefficient nurse. His wife did the scheduling and billing from the back room. The doctor recorded his patient notes in longhand. No matter when you called—even on holidays—he answered the phone himself. If there was no cure, he made one up—like rubbing a potato on your warts, throwing it over your shoulder, and burying it in your backyard (Jennifer trusted him so much she insisted on doing this). After he died, we never found a replacement.

These memories are of a simpler time in medicine. Back then, most physicians were self-employed and practiced out of their homes. Today, as our health care system becomes more complex and interdependent, other types of employment and practice settings predominate. In the future, we can expect even more changes in where and how physicians practice medicine.

In Chapter 1, we asked you to envision yourself as a physician. Recall the setting in which you imagined yourself practicing medicine. Now ask yourself, Is this a practical option for physicians today or in the future? Most of you will probably not picture yourselves hanging out a shingle on the front of your home. On the other hand, you might not conceive of the possibility of commuting an hour each way to a modern twenty-floor health care facility staffed by hundreds of other physicians.

Even if you are clear about your practice goals, the reality is that many factors, including choice of specialty, will determine your employment opportunities and type of practice. If you specialize in emergency medicine, for example, you are opting to work in a hospital or clinic, usually in a salaried arrangement. If you become a primary care physician, you will find the largest number of employment opportunities in health maintenance organizations (HMOs).

In turn, your practice setting dictates various features of your daily work: work hours, autonomy, level of stress, diversity and volume of patients, responsibility for finances, and support of colleagues. For example, physicians who work in a teaching hospital work largely in teams and have the opportunity to stay current with the latest medical developments and research. Physicians in private practice (individual or small group) are usually better paid but more isolated. So part of the choice you make in becoming a physician is not only about what you do as a physician but under what working conditions you do it.

Another choice you will face as you begin to practice is between a salaried arrangement and self-employment.

In order to have more balance between their personal and professional lives, many physicians are moving from self-employment to employee status. The appeal of being a salaried physician is more predictable income, work that consumes fewer hours per week, and relief from administrative responsibilities. As an employee, physicians may receive benefits packages such as paid vacations, retirement plans, paid malpractice insurance, and relocation assistance.

Part-time practice is another consideration and is increasingly an option for physicians who have dual-career families, wish to spend more time raising a family, or simply want to have a less frenetic lifestyle.

PRIVATE PRACTICE

Private practice includes working alone (solo practice) or working in a group practice with one or more other physicians.

Solo Practice

The solo practice of medicine, however romantic, is a steadily waning phenomenon; less than half of all physicians are now in solo practice. Whether you buy an existing practice or start your own, the start-up costs of medical practice can be very high, and it can be some time before a new solo practitioner even begins to meet office expenses. Time demands, the stress of learning to run a business (something you never learned in medical school!), and the isolation of working alone can be wearing for the solo practitioner.

You will have more control as a solo practitioner—over choosing your staff and office procedures, for example, or making treatment decisions—but this control comes at the cost of less time off, fewer opportunities for collegial interaction and consultation, and no income if you need to take time off for illness or family business. However, many patients believe the solo practitioner provides more personalized and better care.

Group Practice

Today, there is a trend toward shared practices. The average size of a group practice is eleven physicians, but some are smaller and some are megagroups with more than one hundred physicians. Group practices can be single-specialty or multispecialty. They can be independently run by the physician-owners or managed by a management service organization (an organization that provides office services and handles the business side of your practice).

In a group practice, the physician can get advice and support from associates, the business costs and paperwork burdens are shared, and there is more flexibility in scheduling responsibilities. You can subspecialize and develop expertise in a particular area without treating the whole spectrum of patient problems related to your specialty. On the other hand, you will give up some independence to be a member of the group, will need to share decision-making responsibilities about the business side of your practice, and may have differences of opinion with other members of your practice over medical philosophy or treatments. If your practice is under a management service organization, you will have access to management expertise and operating capital but will have less control than you would in an independent group practice.

Other practice structures are possible today. There are independent practice associations, specialty care networks and multispecialty networks, and variations on these arrangements—all with positive and negative aspects.

HOSPITAL-BASED PRACTICE

The traditional hospital-based specialties are anesthesiology, emergency medicine, pathology, and radiology. However, options in hospital-based practice are expanding.

There are many different types of hospital-based practices and arrangements. You can be based in a community hospital, government-sponsored hospital, teaching hospital, children's hospital, or a hospital that focuses on one area of medicine, such as an orthopedic hospital.

A hospital-based practice can be structured as a private group practice under contract with the hospital, where you retain some autonomy, or it can be structured like an HMO, where you function more like an employee of the hospital. Increasingly, hospitals are purchasing group practices, particularly primary care practices, in order to attract the physicians' patients and get managed care contracts. Under this arrangement, your fate for better or for worse can be tied to that of the hospital.

AMBULATORY CARE SETTINGS

An ambulatory care setting is one in which the patient ambulates (gets in and out in one day). This includes both hospital-based and free-standing (non-hospital-based) clinics or urgent care centers for minor emergencies. For example, if you break your rib playing basketball at night (as Jennifer's father did recently), you might prefer to go to one of these centers, which have evening hours and handle minor emergencies, rather than to your family physician or an emergency room in a hospital.

Many surgical specialists, particularly ophthalmologists, own or work in ambulatory settings. Surgical procedures typically done in an ambulatory setting include hernia repair, cataract surgery, colonoscopy, and breast biopsy. Some ambulatory settings are highly specialized; one well-known clinic, for example, only deals with the surgical repair of inguinal hernias.

In an ambulatory setting, you will rarely see the same patient twice and therefore won't have the relationships you would have with long-term patients. Your facility will be better equipped than the typical private office but probably not as well equipped as a hospital. On the positive side, you will be paid a salary regardless of patient volume and can set your own schedule.

HEALTH MAINTENANCE ORGANIZATIONS (HMOs)

HMOs are the prototypical design of managed health care in the nation; the largest and best known of these is Kaiser Permanente. An HMO may include relatively few physicians or be a comprehensive nationwide organization with thousands of physicians. Since the emphasis of an HMO is on preventive health and outpatient care, the majority of physicians working for HMOs are in primary care.

In the last decade, the number of individuals enrolled in HMOs has more than tripled. As a result, the number of physicians working for HMOs is also increasing. Currently, over half of all physicians have contracts with an HMO.

The advantages of working for an HMO are multiple. At a staff model HMO, you are released from many of the financial and other responsibilities of running a medical practice. You have a guaranteed steady income (a salary), relatively predictable work hours, less paperwork, and limited on-call responsibilities. In addition, you have a large and diverse patient population and an extended network of physicians with whom you can collaborate. Many physicians find that HMO employment offers a saner, less stressful lifestyle.

In return for these benefits, physicians may sacrifice some control over how they practice medicine. Physicians in HMOs typically follow treatment protocols, may be limited in their referrals, and usually see a greater volume of patients, which makes for quicker and often more impersonal care.

GOVERNMENT PRACTICE

A variety of medical practice opportunities are available through state and federal agencies. The advantage of working in a government setting includes a stable salary and benefits, regular work hours, and opportunities to work on a particular research project or with a particular type of patient without the concerns of running the business side of practicing medicine. There are also possibilities to work in special projects around the world. In the commissioned corps of the Public Health Service, for example, a physician may work in the United States or with the World Health Organization (WHO) in underserved areas around the world. Other possibilities include working for the Centers for Disease Control, the Food and Drug Administration (which often hires physician-lawyers), the Foreign Service, and the Veterans Administration.

MILITARY PRACTICE

The U.S. Air Force, U.S. Navy, and U.S. Army provide various ways to pursue a medical career in the military. Military practice offers many of the benefits of government practice in general. In addition, undergraduates can get financial assistance for medical school if they commit to a specified period of time as a military physician after completing their studies. There are also opportunities to do residency training and medical practice in the military. Navy physicians can get training in undersea medicine, for example, and the Air Force provides training in flight-related disorders. The Army has world-famous research facilities such as Walter Reed Army Hospital in Washington, D.C.

You can also work with the military Reserves or National Guard, either full-time or (more often) part-time, for an extra source of income, for example, one weekend a month and a two-week summer camp, unless you're called up to active duty.

ACADEMIC PRACTICE

This practice arrangement occurs in a medical school with an affiliated hospital, where faculty can focus on their area of expertise such as basic science, research, or clinical work. Many academic appointments include teaching, clinical work and supervision, obtaining grants and conducting research, and involvement in scholarly endeavors like publishing and lecturing.

Some physicians combine private practice with a part-time or adjunct academic appointment. In a way, this can be the best of both worlds—some teaching and mentoring of medical students to offset the demands of seeing patients or doing surgery.

Increasingly, some full-time positions in academic medicine are totally clinical. With a clinical faculty appointment you assume full-time responsibility for patient care and provide supervision for residents or medical students rotating through your service. You do not, however, assume instructional responsibilities other than this supervision.

TEMPORARY PRACTICE POSITIONS

Suppose you finish your residency and aren't ready to settle down in one location or practice arrangement. That's when you can take advantage of temporary practice options.

Locum tenens employment involves taking over another physician's practice for a period of time (months or years) and then returning this practice to the original physician when the contracted time is completed. The salary is guaranteed, and you get to experience various practice and lifestyle options before making your own long-term commitment. There are many *locum tenens* placement firms that can assist you in finding the best arrangement and location to suit your needs.

Another option would be to work in a foreign country—usually a developing country—for a specified period of time under the sponsorship of a philanthropic, nonprofit, or religious organization. These positions typically offer living arrangements and a small salary as well as the psychic rewards of providing much-needed health care to underserved populations.

You can also find temporary practice opportunities in special projects such as Project USA, an American Medical Association (AMA) program that recruits physicians for short-term service in rural areas. For a listing of addresses for the AMA and other medical organizations, see Appendix D. For World Wide Web pages and other on-line information about medicine, see Appendix E.

NONCLINICAL CAREERS
IN MEDICINE

Society expects a physician to be a clinician and, in fact, most physicians choose a clinical career. But you must decide for yourself what you enjoy in medicine and what you want out of life.

Physicians go into nonclinical careers for diverse reasons: some want to use their medical background for another career, such as writing; some want to become involved in health care policy decisions; some want management positions, for example, director of a university health service; some want more involvement with cutting-edge medicine through research; some simply feel they can make a contribution elsewhere, such as advocating for health care reform.

Some physicians will opt for a nonclinical career as a midlife career change. Others can maintain a foot in both worlds by having part-time careers in both clinical and nonclinical settings.

The ratio of physicians in clinical versus nonclinical careers has remained constant over the past few decades: about 20 percent of all physicians are in nonclinical careers. For some nonclinical careers, a Ph.D., M.P.H, or J.D. degree will be necessary in addition to the M.D. or D.O. degree.

We mention nonclinical options so that you may be aware of the range of alternatives in medicine. You should know, however, that many of these careers do not require an M.D. or D.O. degree. There may be more direct ways to enter these professions than through the lengthy process of going to medical school.

Administrator

An increasing number of physicians will be in administrative or managerial positions in the future because of larger specialty practices and the way medicine will be organized. Hospital management firms need administrators with medical expertise. Large corporations often employ medical directors to run their medical departments. Pharmaceutical and research firms may use physicians in administrative roles. Medical schools employ physicians not only as faculty but also as deans and other administrators. Charitable organizations or foundations may use physician-administrators to award grants or oversee scientific research.

When we consider the ways medicine is changing—for example, telemedicine systems can provide consultation around the world by transmitting images over standard telephone lines—it is easy to envision health settings where physicians would perform an administrative role.

Responsibilities as an administrator can be extensive. For example, the medical director of an emergency medical system would be responsible for emergency medical technicians and paramedics, overseeing medical aspects of the system, and maintaining relationships with physicians and hospitals in the community.

Research Scientist

For some physicians, research is very appealing because it is intellectually rigorous and cuts across many disciplines, such as physiology, pharmacology, or molecular biology. Usually the M.D. and Ph.D. degrees are required for research positions in academic, pharmaceutical, or other research settings. Some medical schools have special programs for students who are interested in careers as physician-scientists.

Consultant

A physician can become a full- or part-time consultant on medical issues to various corporations or organizations, law firms, insurance companies, or the media.

Other nonclinical careers that physicians enter are medical publishing, program or policy planning (in private foundations or the government), medical equipment sales, or clinical pharmacology.

PART TWO

THE PRE-MEDICAL YEARS

5

CHOOSING YOUR UNDERGRADUATE SCHOOL

When thinking about an undergraduate institution, it's tempting to go for the school that you think will give you the best chance of getting into medical school. Unfortunately, there's no guarantee that a particular school will give you a better shot at getting into medical school than another. Even if you could find the special school that increases your chances of getting into medical school, think beyond this motive for choosing a college.

College can and should do more for you than give you an impressive transcript. It can mold you as a person, provide involvement with a community, and offer a wealth of experiences you might not have otherwise. A college education is the foundation on which you build the rest of your life. Don't shortchange yourself by making a misinformed or hasty decision.

So what *is* important in choosing a college? Well, what do you *want* from your college experience? First, you need to consider the quality of the academic curriculum and educational experiences. Then, you want to think about the environment in which you will be living and learning for the next few years. You need to think about the type of people who will be your peers and your professors, the quality of student resources and activities, and the overall learning environment.

All the medical students we interviewed talked about college as a turning point in their lives. But each person sought something different from the college experience:

- Ali appreciated the close interaction with his professors in small classes.
- Elena wanted a college that allowed flexibility in the academic curriculum and the chance to take independent study classes.
- Facika wanted an environment that encouraged cooperation rather than competition among students.
- Huong appreciated the opportunity to do service-oriented work.
- James discussed the importance of a pre-medical advisor and academic support services.

Choosing an undergraduate school is difficult because you have such a breadth of options. Even at the same college, students can have vastly different experiences. There isn't a perfect choice for all pre-medical students. But if you know what you want from your college experience, you'll at least have an idea what to look for in a school.

WHAT MAKES A DIFFERENCE IN A COLLEGE?

Your parents may have one idea about what's important in a college, while your high school guidance counselor or best friend has another.

Ultimately, though, it's up to you. What are *your* priorities? Do you feel comfortable in a large university? Would you benefit from an all-women's college? Would you be happy in a military-style dorm room? Are you looking for any out-of-the-ordinary experiences such as service work, senior thesis, or third year abroad?

This is your opportunity to get the most—not just from academics but from your life. Let's take a look at some factors that can make a difference in your college experience. When visiting schools, reading catalogs, and meeting with faculty and students, keep in mind your priorities for your education.

Reputation of the College

Most students put a high priority on the academic reputation of the college they plan to attend. Still, you need not attend a big-name school to get a good education. In fact, sometimes reputation can exceed quality in areas you value. If you want a learning environment that is small and interactive, an overcrowded lecture hall at a prestigious Ivy League school might not satisfy you. Or maybe a school has an excellent choice of classes and professors, but the classes are all closed by the time you register. Look beyond the label to see what you're really getting in a school.

Size of the School

There are advantages to both large and small schools. Some smaller liberal arts institutions can give you an excellent education, close faculty–student relationships, and study-abroad programs. Smaller private institutions often have more student body diversity than most state institutions, which must take a certain percentage of state residents. Larger institutions, although they can be impersonal, can offer you rich on-campus resources and an array of elective courses.

Two factors involved in the large versus small school question are class size and faculty–student ratio. These tell you whether the instructor is just a speck in front of a thousand heads in a large auditorium or someone you may get to know personally. Make sure any cited ratio specifies the *undergraduate* faculty–student ratio. Graduate courses are always smaller, and including them in the statistics can be misleading.

Always check how easy it will be for you to get into the classes you want or need. At some large state universities, students sometimes may have difficulty registering for the courses they need when they want to, thus delaying graduation or timing for the MCAT.

Pre-medical Academic and Support Services

All schools have some academic and support services, but quality differs. Several schools gear their programs to pre-medical students. They even have for-credit classes to prepare you for the Medical College Admissions Test (MCAT), seminars on the application process, and mock interviews. It's not necessary to go this route—to have a pre-medical program laid out for you from the beginning. But you should look into the existence and quality of classes you'll need for medical school and resources that may ease your burdens as a pre-med student. Some questions to consider are listed in the box on the next page.

Assessing Pre-medical and Academic Support Services

Does the school offer the courses necessary for medical school admission?

Are these courses well taught and easily accessible?

How available are faculty members to students?

What sort of academic support services are offered (e.g., tutoring, learning centers, or counseling)?

How good are the medical school advising services?

Is the pre-medical advisor a member of the faculty and involved with the student community?

Is this person in communication with medical schools and up-to-date with the information?

Are there activities and events for pre-medical students?

Are there opportunities for volunteer health work?

Are there adequate application support services (medical school information, letters of recommendation file service, or mock interviews)?

What percentage of students get into medical school?

On what criteria is this percentage based? (Some schools can inflate the statistics by rigorous preselection of students they recommend for medical school.)

Does the school offer a combined B.S./M.D. degree program? What are the advantages to you of considering such a program?

Mission of the School

The school's mission is a reflection of what the administration, the faculty, and the students value. For example, a school may focus on the liberal arts, on science and technology, or on an alternative educational approach such as service learning. Some schools are primarily research institutions; others concentrate on undergraduate teaching. A research university receives a substantial amount of federal money to support research and development activities. These schools offer comprehensive programs in many fields at the master's and doctoral levels.

You may be attracted to a large research university by big-name faculty. Regrettably, some of the best scholars are also the most elusive, particularly to undergraduates. Check out your chances of having these people as instructors in your classes. Will you ever get the opportunity to work on a research project with any of these well-known people? Moreover, what are your chances as an undergraduate of working with *any* faculty on research projects?

The school's mission will affect what you learn and how you learn. Later in this book, we discuss our bias toward the liberal arts as preparation for life—and medical school (see Chapter 6).

Cost of the School and Financial Assistance

Don't be discouraged from applying to a college simply because of financial factors. All schools offer scholarships and loans. In fact, an expensive private school may have campus-based financial aid that makes it equal or less in cost than a public school. Check out the financial aid office of the school where you plan to attend, and apply early for financial assistance if you need it.

Scholarships are wonderful, if you can get one. The cold reality for most students is loans, work-study, or both. Be realistic about how much you can work and still do well in school.

If you plan to use loans to finance both undergraduate and medical education, consider the effect of this debt on your ultimate lifestyle and freedom a dozen years from now.

Location and Environment

Some students are anxious to get away from home, to be independent in a new and far-off place, while others need to be close to family. Other factors may be important: Do you like warm weather, an urban environment, or a place of natural beauty?

You should be able to imagine yourself in the environment of a school—living on campus or commuting, making friends, feeling stimulated or safe, or whatever it is that makes a living environment ideal for you. Spend some time at the college you are considering. Look at the school's offering of social and cultural activities. See if there are enough places and people on campus that pique your interest, or if you feel bored and uncomfortable. Get a sense of where you fit in.

Some students attend a college in the state where they wish to attend medical school, to establish residence and increase their chances of acceptance. As states make more stringent residence laws, this is becoming more difficult.

You can answer some of your questions about a school from the catalog, written materials, or the school's home page on the World Wide Web. But remember, the school's public image in catalogs and other media will be the best one they can project. To really have your questions answered, you must visit the school in person.

VISITING THE CAMPUS

You should visit any school you are seriously considering. Don't simply do the usual formal campus tour and meetings with faculty and staff, but talk with students, hang out in the student union, stay overnight in the dorm, browse the library, eat in the cafeteria, poke in and out of classes. Leave your parents back in the motel after the formal part of the visit so you can blend in with other students and not be given the special visitor treatment.

When you visit, keep three general questions in mind:

Will I have a good chance for academic success in this environment?

Will I be satisfied living and learning in this environment?

How comfortable will I be with faculty and students in terms of values, background, goals, and interests?

Attend some classes. Are students raising their hands to answer questions, or pinching themselves to stay awake? Ask students how easy it is to register for classes.

Check out the student housing—how comfortable and attractive is it? Are there honors dorms or living and learning centers at the institution? What are the criteria for admission to these programs? What are the housing options off-campus?

Think about the quality of life on campus for all students (e.g., minority, gay or lesbian, or students with disabilities). Do students self-segregate in the cafeteria or dorms? Are there tensions among groups? How is the university administration handling diversity issues?

Each school has something distinctive to offer, whether it's course offerings, diversity of the student body, opportunities for independent study, or community service possibilities.

WHAT IF I CHOSE
THE WRONG COLLEGE?

Many of you reading this are already in college or have completed your undergraduate education. What if you didn't take the undergraduate requirements most medical schools require? What if your current institution isn't preparing you properly?

It's never too late to start over, even if you have to back up and choose a new path. Jennifer started college as a chemistry major at a relatively small state university. She benefited from caring and creative faculty and a more personal environment. At the end of her sophomore year, she left this school that she loved, but felt she had outgrown, for a large research university. Three years at this research university provided her with other opportunities, but only because she actively sought involvement in an otherwise impersonal and anonymous environment.

POSTBACCALAUREATE
PRE-MEDICAL PROGRAMS

What if you have completed college and now are considering medical school? If you don't have the academic course requirements for medical school admission, a formal nondegree program may be for you. Both Anita and Lloyd completed their undergraduate requirements that way: Anita did it through a formal program, and Lloyd did it by picking up the undergraduate courses he needed.

If you want to complete only a few courses and not an entire program, contact the pre-medical advisor or career counseling office at the institution you are interested in attending to see if this is possible.

More than one hundred institutions now offer postbaccalaureate pre-medical programs. Most are not designed to enhance a previous lackluster record but to provide undergraduate courses necessary for medical school admission. Programs typically begin in June and continue through an intense and concentrated academic year.

The best of these programs will offer small classes not available to the typical degree-seeking undergraduate, volunteer experiences in a hospital setting, linkages with medical schools, and support services such as no-cost tutoring, MCAT preparation, and workshops focused on the medical school application.

Some programs focus on certain populations, such as state residents, alumni, underrepresented minorities, women, nontraditional students, individuals in health care professions, or unsuccessful medical school applicants. Some schools require a minimum undergraduate GPA or minimum SAT scores.

The same caveats apply here as to undergraduate institutions: investigate, visit, weigh costs (time and money), speak with students and alumni of these programs, sit in on classes, and decide if you are the type of person who can benefit from the structure and support this type of program can provide.

The Association of American Medical Colleges (AAMC) has an up-to-date listing of formal postbaccalaureate pre-medical programs. Appendix D gives the address of AAMC and other organizations in medicine.

6

LOVING YOUR YEARS AS AN UNDERGRADUATE

In high school, everyone else took care of you. Homework was assigned and checked. Teachers and classes were scheduled for you. You knew you would be in trouble if you were late for sixth-period American History.

In college, all of this changes. You decide what you want to learn and when you learn it. You schedule your classes and your time.

For many students this is the first taste of freedom—and responsibility. What are you going to do with this freedom? You can party till dawn and sleep till noon if that's what you want. But if you are excited about learning, then you need to find a balance between self-indulgence and academic diligence during the college years.

The good news is that you have a lot of options in college. The bad news is that decisions are often harder to make when there are more possibilities (like trying to choose from a menu with seventy-five different entrées). The temptation is to revert to a high school mentality: to let someone else take control or simply follow the wave of everyone around you. There are plenty of students like this: the ones whose parents insisted that they should be doctors, or those who declared a biology major because that is the "right" major for pre-meds. But with this philosophy, why leave high school?

In college you need to make many important decisions not by default but by considering what you want to achieve and what will make you happy.

HAPPINESS AND SUCCESS AS A PRE-MEDICAL STUDENT

Many pre-medical students begin their undergraduate life with the mind-set that to be successful, they have to sacrifice. The pre-medical circuit is loaded with advice on how to get ahead (at any cost): major in engineering, join the speech team, or get an A in Organic Chemistry. What they don't mention is *you*—your happiness, your needs, your life.

Before you obsess about your transcript, ask yourself, What do I want? This should be the first consideration when making decisions about your education. Students who focus exclusively on getting into medical school may lose the most important aspect of the undergraduate years—the process of developing oneself.

Ivan, now a radiologist in a group practice, recalls,

I was constantly being reminded of what it took to get into medical school. People would say, "Oh, medical school, that's tough. You have to get good grades to get into medical school." So I spent all my time and effort thinking of what I could get on my CV [résumé]; what would impress the people on the admissions committee. It was like the acceptance letter was the be-all and end-all. I lost sight of the eventual goal of being a physician.

We're not advising you to disregard admissions standards or requirements—that would be unrealistic. But neither should you neglect your own needs. In fact, what you want for yourself and what medical schools want in their students might not be that different (see the box on the next page).

Pre-medical students often complain that they have to conform to a pre-med stereotype. The truth is, medical schools do not want a group of clones who have sacrificed themselves to accomplish a set of pre-medical prerequisites. While pre-medical culture may encourage conformity, medical schools appreciate diversity in their applicants. The qualities they look for in students—academic achievement, self-awareness, a commitment to medicine—are developed by exploring your own interests and not being afraid to try new experiences.

Comparing Your Goals and Medical Schools' Goals

What I Want	What Medical Schools Want
To explore all facets of myself and develop my abilities	Students with self-awareness who have a passion for finding answers and who excel at what they do
To get a well-rounded education	Students who are broadly educated and academically prepared to handle medical school
To perform well on the MCAT	Students who can do well in a medical school curriculum
Personal growth	Students with maturity, empathy, ability to handle sensitive situations
To make friends, find mentors	Students who have good rapport with people
To make informed and thoughtful decisions about my future	Students with a realistic understanding of medicine as a career

So don't think sacrifice. Think about the person you will be four years from now. You want to be proud of who you are and what you accomplished but you also want to say, "I did it, and I did it in my own way."

HOW TO DO IT YOUR OWN WAY AND SUCCEED

Doing it your own way is possible as long as you know how to maneuver within the system. Think of your pre-medical preparation as having three components: (1) what needs to be done, (2) what should be done, *but in your own way*, and (3) everything else.

Accomplishing what needs to be done is the bare bones of success: taking the classes required for admission, planning your schedule wisely, preparing for the MCAT, and getting good grades. In subsequent chapters, we review techniques to help you manage these tasks. But first we consider those components of your pre-medical preparation that you design: your undergraduate major, health-related work, and community involvement.

Then, of course, you need to continue everything else that you value—eating dinner with family, going to Bible study, or dancing to techno music as the sun rises. Pursuing what you love in the pre-medical years and maintaining a balanced life are just as important as your student responsibilities.

MAKING DECISIONS
FOR YOUR PRE-MEDICAL YEARS

Planning your pre-medical years requires a lot of foresight and thought. The following tips will help you make wise and timely decisions about your education.

DON'T LIMIT YOUR OPTIONS
Most of us limit our options before we make a decision. We say, "I have to major in biology" or "I have to find a research job" before we examine all the possibilities.

The theologian Dietrich Bonhoeffer once wrote, "The weak are always forced to decide between alternatives they have not chosen themselves." This is a very human tendency: to play it safe, to take what is given to us, to stick with what is known. As a pre-medical student, it is easy to fall into this pattern: a predetermined schedule of classes, expected activities, or even the choice of friends.

Pre-medical programs tend to maintain a structure. Remember though, just because you are provided with options A, B, and C doesn't mean that D, E, and F are not possible. Imagine other possibilities—designing your own major or doing an independent study in an area that interests you.

DON'T PROCRASTINATE WHEN YOU NEED TO MAKE DECISIONS
There are several reasons why we put off decisions. First, we aren't sure what we want. So we take more time to think it over. Or we don't

want to make the wrong decision and regret it afterward. So we wait for the perfect decision. Or we want to avoid responsibility. So we try not to think about the decision. Meanwhile, precious time escapes.

When you delay making decisions, your options diminish. If you put off deciding what you want to do for the summer, you wind up in June with few choices. It's good to be analytical, but you shouldn't become paralyzed by the need to make perfect decisions.

Sometimes you have to be lighthearted. While each choice you make affects your life, a single decision rarely casts your life in stone. If you make a mistake, you can go back and redirect your course.

KNOW YOUR OBJECTIVES, ANTICIPATE THE OUTCOME
With each decision, you should ask yourself, What am I after? Consider summer employment. Each of us has different goals: to make money, gain certain skills, or simply to enjoy the summer.

Suppose you have been offered a job working as a medical research assistant at home. At the same time, your best friend wants you to live at the beach and rent rafts. Your decision rests on your priorities.

Once you establish what you want, you need to anticipate the results. How much would you enjoy working at the raft stand? What skills might you gain working as a research assistant?

Consider the decision Ali, now a second-year medical student, made about a summer job in college. Even though most of his friends were doing research for the summer, he decided he wanted to do something different. His goals were to make money and to be able to read. So he got a job as a security guard where he could sit at his post all night and read philosophy and literature. He knew what he wanted, and he found a way—however unorthodox—to make that work.

DECISION ONE: THE MANY PATHS OF EDUCATION

As you learn more about the university and yourself, you will get a better idea of what you want out of your education and how to go about getting it. Above all, you should keep an open mind and be willing to explore all your options.

Undergraduate Major: Science or Nonscience?

Many students interested in medicine plan to major in pre-medicine. In fact, there is no such major at most universities. Years ago, students who declared themselves pre-med would almost always major in a basic science.

Today, as a pre-medical student, you can choose from hundreds of majors. Elena, now a medical student, was fascinated by biology for many years. She saw it as an active process of exploration and discovery. Huong, on the other hand, felt bogged down by the memorization that biology required. She knew that she would study the sciences in medical school, and she wanted to pursue another area in her undergraduate years, so she did a double major in psychology and creative writing.

One advantage of majoring in the sciences is that the classes you take for your major overlap with the basic science requirements of most medical schools. Nonscience majors need to do some extra work to fulfill these requirements (see Chapter 7).

As far as medical schools are concerned, your major is not as important as how well you do in your major—what your grades are. Pre-medical students often feel they have to major in biology or chemistry to be competitive candidates for medical school. And yet, surprisingly, the highest rate of acceptance to medical school is for philosophy majors!

The appeal of a nonscience major is more diversity in your day-to-day routine. In the morning you may learn about platelet clots; in the afternoon you do a literary analysis of *The Canterbury Tales*. This mix of knowledge is an opportunity you may not have again—certainly not in medical school. Ivan recognized this in retrospect:

> At the time, I didn't think that going into an area outside of the sciences would be smart. Now, I look back and think I kind of wish I had majored in something unrelated, like drama or literature. I know some of my friends in medicine who did that in their undergraduate years, and I think that they got a lot out of those years.

Facika believes that studying the humanities allowed her to step outside of her own value system and to understand people. This also affected how she related with fellow students, her professors, and people of different cultures. The humanities gave her a different perspective on science:

> I realized that science is only valuable in the backdrop of humanity. If you make a scientific discovery—well, so what? The point is, How is this going to affect people?

A warning: If you are a nonscience major, you will need to be vigilant about your pre-medical science preparation. You must demonstrate by your performance in academic course work that you can handle the rigors of a medical school curriculum. In addition, nonscience majors are usually outside the pre-med circuit. You may see this as a blessing, but remember, you will have to go further to inform yourself of the activities and services that most other pre-meds hear about by word-of-mouth.

THINKING OVER YOUR CHOICE OF MAJOR

Before choosing a major, ask yourself a few questions:

> What subjects do I enjoy?
> What do I do well in?
> How will this major prepare me for medicine?
> If I don't go into medicine, are there other opportunities in this
>   major that appeal to me?
> Can I be happy with the lifestyle and amount of work that this
>   major requires?
> Are there a good number and diversity of classes in this major?
> Are the faculty members in this area well qualified, committed to
>   teaching, and accessible to students?

WHAT TYPE OF EDUCATIONAL BACKGROUND
DO MEDICAL SCHOOLS PREFER?

Today, medical schools are placing more emphasis on a liberal arts education. They want students, whether they major in science or nonscience, to have a breadth of course work spanning disciplines: the natural sciences (biology, chemistry, math), the social sciences (sociology, anthropology, psychology), and the humanities (literature, art, history).

The commitment to liberal arts in the pre-medical curriculum is backed by recent changes in admissions practices of medical schools.

Some schools have reduced science requirements for admission. In 1991 a new MCAT was introduced with an emphasis on critical thinking and problem solving rather than rote science recall. Special admissions programs, like FlexMed at Johns Hopkins, provide early acceptance and delayed enrollment to encourage students to broaden their educational experiences in the senior year and after graduation before entering medical school.

WHAT DO THE LIBERAL ARTS OFFER SOMEONE WHO WANTS TO BE A PHYSICIAN?

The value of the liberal arts in becoming an educated individual is evident. Their role in the practice of medicine may not be as clear. Medicine has long been considered a scientific discipline—the science of human body function. Yet the practice of medicine is not simply the practice of science.

I still remember the words of a physician who spoke to my first-year medical class at orientation. "Before you are a physician, you must first be a human being," she said. "*Human being* is not a noun. It is a verb: *human BEING*." She went on to detail the daily responsibilities of a physician: human watching, human touching, human being aware.

This physician was speaking of the *healing* aspects of medicine. The art of healing requires more than a quick mind and exhaustive knowledge of the body. It also requires a special kind of human awareness. You must be aware of your communication: the meaning of your words or the ways that unstated power (who has it and who doesn't) can affect communication. You must be aware of social realities: recognizing that a child is being abused, or realizing that a person is without money to continue treatment and is too ashamed to tell you. Most important, you must be aware of yourself.

K. Danner Clouser, a professor at Penn State University College of Medicine, believes that certain qualities of the mind evolve through exposure to the humanities. In an article in the *Journal of Medicine and Philosophy* (see References and Suggested Readings), he describes how one quality, "flexibility of perspective," is developed:

> Seeing the human body through the eyes of the artist; study-ing the concept of disease through the categories of an histo-rian; understanding suffering through the views of a theolo-gian; analyzing knowledge claims through the conceptual

tools of a philosopher—these break the shackles of a single vision, goal, method, and focus. Taken together, these are what can keep us limber of imagination and perspective. (p. 295)

Elena talks about her liberal arts education, particularly her first exposure to modern literary criticism. While she took classes in biology, she was studying Lacan and Foucault. She says, "I would walk home from lecture thinking, 'Oh, my God, everything I think could be shattered.'" She describes these moments in her education as being like a wedge opening her mind to things she hadn't seen before.

Having a flexibly trained mind is valuable in medicine when you need to be logical one moment and imaginative the next. Medicine requires a constant shifting of perspective. In a way, it's a combination of being a scientist, a detective, and an artist.

Beyond Classes: Research, Independent Academic Work, and the Academic Community

In college, every moment is potential learning time. Think of the campus as an extended classroom. Imagine that anyone can be your teacher (including yourself). If you can approach your education in this way, you'll get more out of it than if you limit yourself and your learning to simply sitting through lectures.

The following are some areas where you may broaden your education.

RESEARCH

As a pre-medical student, you may assist a professor with basic science or clinical research. You inevitably begin with the "scut work" (making preparations, cleaning test tubes), but you assume more responsibility with time and experience.

Some students get academic credit for their work. James, like many students, did research as part of a class and received nine credit hours toward his degree.

Some students go on to do independent research projects. If you major in political science, you may investigate the political organization of migrant grape workers in California. Instead of the lab, you do research in the library or in the field (conducting surveys, doing interviews).

Research, whether in the basic sciences, social sciences, or other areas, requires the use of the scientific method. You develop skills in problem solving and the presentation of ideas that are valuable for life.

James contends that doing research taught him what it is like "not to know the answers." He learned that no knowledge, not even science, is completely objective or ideal.

Gaining experience with the joys and frustrations of research is particularly important for pre-medical students. After all, research is a vital part of medicine, whether it be epidemiological research, clinical trials, or basic science.

INDEPENDENT ACADEMIC WORK

The option of doing independent study means that you can still learn about Taoism in China even if you cannot find a class on the subject. Or maybe a class already exists, but you want to do something on your own or more in depth, like study the teachings of Lao-tzu.

Independent study is self-directed learning, but with the benefit of a formal academic environment. You may plan your own project or get together with friends to create a class. A faculty member serves as your sponsor and provides guidance and a final evaluation of your work.

When she was an undergraduate, Elena created a course in women's health that required finding a sponsor, developing a reading list, and finding resources. Topics ranged from the depiction of women's bodies in the media to the biology of cervical cancer.

We encourage every student to design at least one independent study project in their undergraduate years. To only take classes that are formally offered in the school catalog is like walking into a fully equipped kitchen and always going for a frozen TV dinner. It's easier, but it is not nearly as enjoyable and stimulating as a project that you personally create.

THE ACADEMIC COMMUNITY

As a college student, you have access to all the social, political, and artistic activity of the university. This is part of your extended classroom: academic conferences, art shows, music performances, and more.

Participating in the academic community is what transforms you from a run-of-the-mill student into a scholar. Instead of preparing a poem for class, you present your work at a poetry reading. Instead of dragging yourself out of bed for lecture, you attend a night symposium on the political history of the Middle East. In the morning, over a cup of coffee, you talk about chromosomal abnormalities and your research on recombinant DNA with a professor.

DECISION TWO:
HEALTH-RELATED WORK

In Chapter 1, we asked you to imagine yourself doing the work of a physician. As an undergraduate, you are able to experience some of this work. If you are working in an Emergency Room, you find out what it is like to be around people who are very ill and frightened. You confront the everyday dilemmas that a physician faces. You get a sense of how you fit into this world.

This is the most important result, from the point of view of a medical school: a realistic appraisal of medicine in relation to your own capabilities. The following are a few types of health-related work you may undertake.

Volunteer Preceptorships

This type of work entails "shadowing" a physician as he or she goes about the normal activities of the day. The physician serves as your mentor. You gain exposure to diagnosis and treatment in an acute care or an ambulatory setting. The best place to do this type of work is in a hospital that is not associated with a medical school, because the physicians are not busy teaching medical students. Most hospitals have volunteer offices. You also may try community clinics or even a doctor's private practice, depending on the type of experience you are seeking.

Volunteer Patient Work

In these volunteer activities, you spend most of your time with patients. Nursing homes and hospices are often desperately in need of volunteers to help with the physical care of patients or simply to lend an ear. Or you may work with others in need: for example, people with chronic illnesses or abused children.

Public Health Programs

These programs focus on issues of public health and preventive medicine. Your activities may include health education (smoking awareness, alcohol/drug education, safe sex) and also public intervention measures (vaccination programs, needle exchange programs). You may be involved with organizing or actually doing the work. This work experience gives you the larger picture of health care—maintaining the health of society rather than just treating disease in individuals.

Trained/Paid Health Work

Some students obtain formal training so that they may gain more extensive experience and get paid for their work. This includes work as an Emergency Medical Technician (EMT), paramedic, nurses' assistant, or other medical technology jobs. Perhaps the most feasible for students is the EMT certification, which can be done in the evenings and weekends in less than a year and which offers opportunity for summer employment. As an EMT, you may ride along in the ambulance, assist paramedics, and provide medical attention.

International Health Projects

There are many opportunities to be involved in health projects abroad, particularly in developing countries. For example, you might work in a leprosy hospital in a rural area of India, for a midwifery project in the Middle East, or with disabled children in Nicaragua. Most of these positions would be volunteer, and you would have to pay your own travel and living costs (you can usually live with a family). International health experiences give you the opportunity to learn about health care in a different context. A great guide to volunteer service organizations and information sources is *Alternatives to the Peace Corps: A Directory of Third World and U.S. Volunteer Opportunities* (see References and Suggested Readings).

The more exposure you have to health care work, the better—not only to find out if medicine is the career for you but to see what specifically about medicine you enjoy. If you do not like the Emergency Room, it does not necessarily mean that you shouldn't be a physician. You may find another setting more stimulating.

Each experience—good or bad—gives you insight into yourself and other people. You gain an appreciation of what makes a good physician. You may meet a particular physician who will serve as your guide, who can provide valuable advice and support.

You will also gain exposure to the U.S. health care system—the challenges, policy issues, and current ideas for reform. You may even pick up a little knowledge about health and the human body—learn the names of a few bones, the signs of a heart attack, or the consequences of untreated meningitis. You may explore the large intestine with the latest fiberoptics equipment, witness a live birth, or view a brain tumor on a magnetic resonance imaging (MRI) scan. These are experiences that you will remember for the rest of your life.

DECISION THREE:
COMMUNITY INVOLVEMENT

To each of us, community means something different. For some, community means family, friends, or neighborhood; for others, it is a group of people with similar beliefs or common goals.

However we define community, we need to feel connected to other people. We need to be with people in different environments so that we can grow, learn about ourselves, and participate in the world.

Every time we try a new experience, as painful or embarrassing as it may be, something changes inside of us. I was scared stiff the first time I walked into a nursing home to volunteer. I kept wondering what I could talk about with older people. And what happened? Nothing mind-shattering. I learned a little bit about the Korean War. I thought about loneliness. I became more comfortable with a bed pan. But the next time I went back, I didn't feel uneasy. *Something had changed.*

As you might expect, there are no automatic doors to community. You have to look for a community, sometimes even create one. You can start with registered student groups in the school catalog. You can also scan the bulletin boards for flyers announcing activities. Some schools have an organization that connects students with volunteer opportunities outside the university. If not, you'll need to practice your telephone skills.

There are many different outlets for community work. Here are a few you may try.

Teaching

Even as a student, you have a lot that you can <u>teach</u>. Each week, you may understand an equation, sharpen your writing skills, or read a book. The more you learn, the more you have to share with others.

Not only that, but the more you teach, the better you understand the material. One student we know worked as a teaching assistant in General Chemistry. Before a class, she'd review the material and think of new ways to explain a concept to the students. More than once, they stumped her with a question during class. By the time the MCAT came around, she had mastered the material. She had helped herself by helping others.

Social Groups

One advantage of a big university is that no matter how unusual your interests, you can always find someone who likes the same thing. Interested in medieval jousting? Like to cook? How about ballroom dancing?

Getting involved with social groups provides a way to meet people (who jousts alone?). It is also a way to keep up with the things that you love or to try out new experiences. (You do not have to be an expert in Middle East cuisine to enjoy the food!)

Then, there are groups that bring together people from a common background—women's collectives, the Native American Student Alliance, the Jewish Student Union. Being a part of these groups reminds you of who you are: your culture, your language, and your personal struggles. These groups are an invaluable source of affirmation and support.

Political Action Groups

Entering the university, you may be a little wishy-washy about your political beliefs. It won't be long, however—amid clashes of opinions and debating dogmas—that you develop a point of view about your immediate surroundings and society. This may come from the simple frustration of watching hundreds of aluminum cans being hauled off to the landfill, or from a run-in with intolerance or bigotry.

Political action groups force you to define your values, first to yourself and then to others. At some point, each of us has to take a stand on issues, whether to keep down educational fees at the university or to take a position on health care reform.

Being able to think critically and to communicate is essential to the work of a physician. As a doctor, you will work with others in a medical team setting. If you believe that a treatment approach is wrong or if you run into an ethical impasse, you can't be afraid to present your point of view.

Advising/Counseling

The most difficult lessons we learn are through experience. Advising is one way of giving others the benefit of our experience. It is as easy as saying, "Yeah, I've been there" or "Yeah, I care."

James, for example, advised minority elementary and high school students about how to prepare for college. By sharing his experience and solutions to problems, he was able to help them develop self-esteem, learn a skill, or cope with a problem.

Counseling is different from advising because we must actively listen and help others find their own answers. Counselors also must be nonjudgmental. Both qualities will take you far in life, particularly as a physician.

Sports/Recreation

How often do you hear it—"teamwork, teamwork." Certainly that's what counts, not only in sports but also as a physician.

But let's forget about that. Sometimes, you have to just let go, to relieve stress, to get your mind off your concerns. Sometimes, you want to sweat—sliding into home base or at the end of a five-mile jog. The physical, mental, and social benefits are without parallel.

Being involved in organized or individual sports is a way to stay centered. It also teaches discipline, especially when working for a goal.

Writing/Communication

The most obvious outlet for gaining writing experience outside classes is a school publication. You may report on events, or write editorials or essays. Or you may contribute to a literary journal or a political magazine. Other media—radio, TV networks, film—all accept interns.

While learning broadcasting skills may not seem relevant to the average pre-medical student, developing communication skills is. The better we learn to express ourselves, the more easily we can transmit our knowledge and advice to patients.

Dance, Music, Art

There's an Ethiopian saying: "If you can walk, you can dance. If you can talk, you can sing." The only thing you have to lose in unleashing your creative urges is your pride—something you should not be too attached to, anyway. Think of all you have to gain: another form of expression, a release, a different way of connecting to the world. It is also something of yourself that you can give to others.

Often, it is the little things—a song, a painting, or a story—that break through the isolation of illness and provide comfort where medical knowledge cannot. In this way, your creativity will aid your work as a physician.

REMEMBERING YOUR PURPOSE

No decision in these years will be easy. Now is a time of change—of new people, new activities, and new expectations. At times, you will feel overwhelmed and the doubts will set in. How will you keep up your energy when the obstacles seem insurmountable? How do you recover from setbacks?

It helps from time to time to remember your greater purpose, the meaning of your work. In the words of Carlos Casteneda in *The Teachings of Don Juan:* "For me, there is only the traveling on paths that have heart, on any path that may have heart. There I travel, and the only worthwhile challenge is to traverse its whole length."

The path to being a physician has many challenges, uphill stretches, even occasional dead ends. But if you are connected with the "heart" of that path, you will prepare yourself for the journey.

To be able to make that happen, you need to focus on another set of purposes—your personal and academic objectives. Remembering your purpose in this sense means writing down what you want and what needs to get done, and devising strategies to accomplish your objectives. If you can stay connected with your greater purpose and keep sight of the immediate objectives required to bring your dreams to the fore, then you will not only find success but a lot of enjoyment in your undergraduate years.

7

MAXIMIZING YOUR POTENTIAL: SKILLS AND QUALITIES

People often speak of potential as if it were a single entity. They'll say, "She has so much potential ... she can do so much if she puts her mind to it."

We have a different way of looking at potential. First, there is the potential of the environment—in your case, the university. This potential includes everything we discussed in Chapter 6: the possibilities in pre-medical education and the different types of health work and community service that you can do. Second, there is the potential of the individual. This is something that you possess. Your potential includes the possibilities for you to make your own decisions, to love what you do, and to expand your boundaries.

The key to success as an undergraduate is to maximize both types of potential. One contributes to the other. For example, you may select a college that has a great deal to offer you as a pre-medical student. The experiences and knowledge you gain from this environment spur your personal growth. You then return this to your environment by creating ideas or art, teaching another person, or sharing your experiences.

While your environment should be chosen carefully, the most important determinant of success is *you*. Since you are a dynamic person, your potential is also subject to change. To maximize your potential and your chances of success, you should work to develop certain skills and qualities.

SKILL ONE: WORKING THE SYSTEM

Life, in essence, is a system. The system includes everything from how to pay a bill to our relationships with others. We follow certain written and unwritten rules of the system—principles such as fairness, respect, and timeliness.

The same is true of the university. Those who excel in this system are those who know the rules of the system and can work it to their advantage. These are the students who get the scholarships, who know what to study for the test, who manage school and work and have time to spare.

Here's how you do it.

KNOW WHAT IS EXPECTED OF YOU
Certain expectations are placed on pre-medical students. Think of these as the "must do" work of your pre-medical years: keeping a high grade point average, completing graduation and medical school admissions requirements, and performing well on the MCAT. Others will spring up along the way. So, ask yourself periodically, What is required of me? Then plan, plan, plan.

KNOW WHAT YOU WANT
You are right to expect something in return for your efforts, whether a grade, a certain degree of knowledge, or a set of experiences. Part of working the system is getting what you want out of it. To do this, you must be clear about your academic and personal goals.

FIND OUT WHAT'S AVAILABLE (AND USE IT)
When you are a student, all the university resources are at your disposal: libraries, academic tutoring, financial aid, work-study programs, career counseling, and other services (most of them free). To get what you want, avail yourself of these resources—visit your academic advisor each semester, attend seminars, enroll in mentor programs, or whatever else it takes.

SKILL TWO: GOAL SETTING

It is said that those who fail to plan, plan to fail. The first step of any planning process is to set goals. You may say, "I want to be a doctor." But how will you do it? This goal must be followed by specific objectives that will help you to achieve it, for example, taking certain courses, getting good grades, and investigating medical schools and their programs. Finally, you break it down to a daily plan of activities: studying for your physics test, talking with a professor about opportunities for health-related work, and similar undertakings.

Setting goals allows you to define what you want and provides a structure in which you can make it happen. Keeping track of the objectives that will allow you to reach your goal helps you stay motivated. Each time you accomplish a goal, no matter how small, you confirm that, yes, you can do it.

In order to benefit from setting goals, you should follow certain rules.

GOALS SHOULD BE CLEAR, PRACTICAL, AND REALISTIC

The most important principle is to set goals that you can accomplish. If you aim to change the world overnight, you're setting yourself up for failure and disappointment. A more realistic, attainable goal might be, "I want to effect change in my community." The goal also should be clear (specifically how do you want to effect change in your community?) and practical (how will this translate into direct actions in your life?).

GOALS MUST BE SUPPORTED BY A CONCRETE PLAN OF ACTION

If you have doubts about whether a goal is reasonable, look at the support. Is the goal followed by clearly specified objectives? Can these objectives be translated into a work plan that is manageable? If so, then even the most far-reaching goals are possible.

For example, if your goal is to effect change in your community by volunteering at a woman's shelter one day a week, your objectives may include talking with the staff about your plans, rearranging your schedule to have the time to volunteer, and arranging transportation. Then create a daily or weekly "to do" list through which to accomplish these objectives.

ONCE YOU SET GOALS, FOLLOW THROUGH

Think of your goals as more than a statement of what you want; rather, they are a commitment to what you plan to achieve. To do this, you need to consider the work each goal requires *before you commit to it*. Set deadlines to achieve your goals. Once you show you can stick to a plan, you'll begin to believe in yourself and your ability to reach your goals.

GOALS MUST BE CONTINUALLY REASSESSED

If a goal is no longer doable, if it doesn't work with your life, or if it counteracts other more important goals, it may need to be modified or discarded altogether. For example, if your work at the shelter is beginning to interfere with your studies, you may need to cut back your volunteer work to something more reasonable.

You should also evaluate your methods for achieving your goals. Remember, there are many means to the same end. There are dozens of ways that you may help women in the community. If you don't feel satisfied with your work in the shelter, you may decide instead to work with women on campus. The same is true of your schoolwork. There are many different ways to do well in your classes and to prepare for medical school. You need to assess what is right for you.

SKILL THREE: TIME MANAGEMENT AND ORGANIZATION

In order to realize your goals, you need to be able to get things done — stay on top of your schoolwork, meet other responsibilities, and keep up with the things you love.

Time management is the way to do it. If you can manage your time well, all your other skills will synergize. You'll complete your tasks efficiently. You'll plan ahead and devote time to the most meaningful activities. In fact, everything you do will become easier.

If you are one of those people who can't keep track of your schedule, who is always forgetting appointments or losing things, or who procrastinates until the last minute, it's time for a change. These habits will hurt you again and again, and cause you undue anxiety.

You can begin your time management practices in the following ways.

PRIORITIZE BY IMPORTANCE

What gets done, and when do you do it? Each of us sets priorities, whether we realize it or not.

The author Stephen Covey describes two types of high-priority activities: the urgent and the important. The urgent includes activities that we must get done because of deadlines (the term paper due the next morning) or because they can't wait (a fire in the kitchen). The important activities are the ones that are truly integral to our lives. They are the activities we would choose to spend our time on if we had control.

The fact is you do have control. It's simply a matter of prioritizing your time according to importance and minimizing your response to urgency. This means planning ahead—anticipating what you need to accomplish around the bend rather than waiting until it becomes urgent. The less time that you spend putting out fires, the more time you will have for the most productive and valuable work.

MAKE AN ALL-INCLUSIVE "TO DO" LIST

In college, you need to balance many different responsibilities. Consider making a "to do" list with the following categories:

* School
* Friends and family
* Volunteer/community work
* Domestic responsibilities
* Explorations and investigations

The last category—explorations and investigations—is particularly important. In addition to carrying out mundane activities like paying bills or studying for an upcoming exam, you should be anticipating and planning the activities that you want to do (or must do) in three months or even a year, like investigating medical schools or finding funds for a summer project. Consider this an essential responsibility: always to be moving forward.

KEEP A SCHEDULE

For those of you who have never carried a daily agenda, you're in for a treat. A daily agenda book is like a peripheral brain. You don't need to remember all those appointments and deadlines if you have a way to organize them.

Your daily agenda will help you account for each hour. You begin with a blank schedule—168 hours each week. After you block in the basics—classes, studying, work, and other routine activities such as exercise—you have precious little discretionary time. You need to make a conscious choice about how you will spend this time; otherwise it manages to dissipate.

Pull out your "to do" list. Decide what gets done today, tomorrow, or next week. Give yourself sufficient time to complete your work. Use the hour between classes and the thirty minutes on the bus to get small tasks done. And keep your word: if you plan to do something, don't get sidetracked.

KEEP "THINGS" ORGANIZED

No one knew better than Einstein the intimate connection between time and space. The same is true for those of us who spend a good deal of time looking for things—the car keys, our books, the notes from the beginning of the semester.

You need a system for organizing your space and the things in that space. One principle of organization is to only touch an object once and then do something with it. For papers, that's a choice between the file cabinet and the trash can.

When organizing class papers, use those colored plastic file crates and colored hanging file folders. Use a crate and hanging files of one color for each class (e.g., purple for physics, orange for O-Chem). Drop your day's papers, notes, and assignments into the appropriate folder in each file crate at the end of each day.

Keep your personal papers in a separate file crate. That way, when you need your old phone bills, you don't have to mount a full-scale search to locate them. For your personal file, the following folder headings may be helpful:

- Things to do (bills to be paid, forms to fill out, a half-finished letter)
- Things to read (articles, books of interest)
- Things to think about (ideas for a project, schools to visit)
- Receipts (a tuition bill, a stereo warranty, car servicing records)

If you are really hopeless (your "to do" list is lost amidst the piles of dirty clothes on your floor, and the file crates overflow), you should seek professional help. Not a shrink—just a short course in time management and organizing skills. Most schools offer such services (free).

SKILL FOUR: STRESS MANAGEMENT/RELAXATION

Stress is an issue of universal concern for pre-medical students. The environment is competitive, and the workload is heavy. No matter how well you prepare, you are bound to suffer setbacks, frustrations, and disappointments. These well up inside and may manifest themselves in unhealthy ways—decreased performance during exams, relationship problems, even depression.

Most pre-medical students deny stress. They pretend it's not there, and as a result they continue to suffer its effects. It's better to befriend it, to own up to it, and to shrink it down to manageable size. A little bit of stress can make us productive; too much stress can immobilize us. If you find stress cutting into your productivity and sense of well-being, try these antidotes.

RECOGNIZE DESTRUCTIVE HABITS AND ATTITUDES AND CHANGE THEM

Let's take the term paper example, since it is a common one among college students. Do you scramble to finish term papers at 3 A.M. the morning before they are due, each time swearing that *next time* things will be different but committing the same mistake again?

The fact is, most of our stress is of our own doing. It is not the responsibilities in our lives that cause stress as much as our way of handling them. And as most of us know, bad habits tend to become ingrained.

The next time you are in a stressful situation, step back and ask, Why? Isolate what exactly is causing the stress and what steps led to the stressful situation. Probably, you'll realize it's not the term paper but the pressure of writing it at the last minute, which was caused by poor planning and lack of organization.

Once you identify what causes you stress, you can target this behavior for change. But remember, if you resolve that next time will be better, be prepared to follow up with determined effort. Change doesn't come easily.

CLEAR YOUR MIND

While out with friends, do you find yourself thinking about a project for school? Do you drive yourself crazy analyzing your relationships?

You may not realize it, but you're obsessing. If you spent the day in the library getting "nothing" done, what *were* you doing? Watch out for the obsessive time nibblers chewing into your thoughts.

Then go ahead—give yourself permission to "obsess"—but for no more than half an hour per day. You can schedule your "obsessing" time into one block or into three ten-minute blocks. While you are obsessing, ask yourself, What really bothers me about this? Is this something I realistically should be concerned about? What can I do about it? Write down your solutions, so that you come out of your obsessing session feeling focused, not confused and anxious. Then, any other time you find yourself obsessing when it's not your obsessing time, say "Stop! I'll think about that tomorrow morning at 8 A.M., not now."

SEE IT AS IT IS

Many students have a tendency to exaggerate or distort the importance of an event. It seems to be such a huge deal—one test, one misunderstood remark, one situation gone awry. This can lead to habitual anxiety.

Think of the worst outcome of any one event. Perhaps you might say, "If I fail this test, I will never get into medical school." This is obviously an exaggeration; even if you fail a test, it is unlikely that this one event will keep you out of medical school. When you start catastrophizing, change your perception from seeing total disaster to saying, "It is only one event."

LET IT GO

Some events and circumstances that cause anxiety are out of your control—the morning thunderstorm and traffic jam on the way to your exam, the questions you never thought would be asked, or your grade (after you take the exam). To fret over these things would be pointless.

Learn to separate the productive stress (stress that sparks positive change) from nonproductive stress (worrying about things out of your control). Ask yourself, Is this something that I can control? If not, let it go.

FIND A RELEASE

When all else fails, exercise. Studies show that exercise relieves stress and also counters depression. At the very least, it gets your mind off the problem. Relaxation techniques may also help. Some students meditate, get a massage, or practice yoga.

GET HELP

If stress is a real concern for you, look into workshops on stress management at your university. Or you may find it helpful to talk over these issues with a counselor. Check with the Career Center or Psychological Services at your university (again, free).

SKILL FIVE: REWORKING THE SYSTEM

Sometimes, even when you play by the rules, you get stuck. You may plan ahead, but unforeseen circumstances get in your way. Occasionally, the system itself will be the force that's holding you back.

That's when you need to rework the system—to rethink the rules, to broaden your vision, to imagine a different way of doing things. This may be difficult to do from inside a system that appears fixed and unyielding. We forget that these systems, whether they are family units, a culture, or a university, are human constructs.

Just as people create the system, people can change it. In fact, if we are to maximize the potential of our environment, we need to be constantly revising the system to make sure that it works, that it adapts to our changes, and that it is responsive to most people.

But how do you do it?

LOOK FOR THE EXCEPTION

Every rule has one, whether it is the requirements to take a certain class, prerequisites for medical school, or the stipulations for financial aid. If you find that something isn't working for you, look for a potential bypass. For example, if you see in the course catalog that you don't have the prerequisites for a class you want, speak with the professor or ask your advisor what might be substituted. You'd be surprised at how many of those "must do"s may actually be "maybe so"s. Just be careful not to depend on this. Try to judge beforehand how far you can push it.

BE THE EXCEPTION

Regardless of how everyone else tells you to do it, you need to follow your own style. This is how art evolves; it's how social structures are reshaped; and it's also how systems change.

By diverging from the norm, you actually change the norm. It was just a short while ago that women didn't apply to medical school. A few stalwart women were the exception. As more and more women became physicians, policies changed. Now almost 40 percent of graduating physicians are women.

CREATE AN ALTERNATIVE

Too often, we invest our energy into gripes and moans about how inadequate or unfair the system is. Instead of whining, find the gumption to create an alternative to what you dislike. For example, a group of students at one university who were tired of buying outrageously priced textbooks and selling them back to the bookstore at a pittance decided to create a student-run cooperative bookstore.

All it takes is a little self-reliance and creativity. If you recognize a need that isn't being met by the system, think of ways that this can be resolved by you. Form a group that shares note-taking responsibility. If you can't get funding for a project, have an independent fundraiser. Not only do you benefit but you leave something behind for others, even if it's only your example.

CULTIVATING POSITIVE QUALITIES

Every now and again, you need to take a long, hard look at yourself. Each of us will find a few rough edges—passivity, wavering self-esteem, or pride. Rather than stumble on with these personal deficiencies, think about what you can do to rise above them.

Don't ever say, "That's just the way I am." None of us are static creatures unless we choose to be so. We need to be open to the possibility of change.

QUALITY ONE: HUMILITY AND HARD WORK

Everyone shrugs at this one—humility. Who is propelled to success by being humble?

In fact, humility is the basis for all self-improvement. To learn, you have to admit that you don't know. In order to become a better person, you need to be able to face your weaknesses. Even to gain a skill, you have to confront a lack of skill.

Yet in our world of boasting and proving, humility can be an uncomfortable shoe to wear. The first time you ask a question in class you may feel embarrassed that you don't understand something. When someone offers you a criticism, you may respond defensively: "It wasn't my fault . . . I didn't know." Such reactions are the face of pride. And the unfortunate price we pay is ignorance, stagnation, and a harder road in the future.

Better to break that beast of pride down early. Practice saying, "I don't know" (good preparation for medical school). Learn to look honestly at yourself. The only thing you can't change is what you can't see or are afraid to admit.

The follow-up to humility is hard work. There is little benefit to being humble if you don't have the will to change. If a teacher explains a physics problem to you, go and do five more just like it. If someone offers you criticism, use this insight to direct personal change.

QUALITY TWO: FOLLOW-THROUGH

Every time we set out to do something, we invest part of ourselves. When we actually follow through, when we complete some work or bring our dreams to fruition, we gain something back—a new vitality, self-confidence, or sense of self-sufficiency.

This is equally true of our promises to others. Only now someone else invests in us. They take our word as a sign of commitment. When we fulfill this commitment, it returns to us as trust, greater responsibility, and independence.

On the other hand, when we renege on our promises, when we abandon a dream, or leave a project by the wayside, a part of us suffers. This manifests itself as uncertainty, self-doubt, or inadequacy.

You won't always be able to finish everything that you start. But even if you fall a little short, the important point is that you have tried and that you learn from the experience. The next time around, you will be clearer about your commitment and what you are able to do.

QUALITY THREE: ASSERTIVENESS

Most of the time, you have to be courageous to get what you want from this life. You track down the people who have what you need. You stand up in the face of injustice. You take risks.

In the university, as in life, you can't wait for opportunity to knock. You have to make it happen on your own. If you have a great idea for a summer project, exhaust every possible resource to obtain funding. If you want to do research, call a professor directly.

At times, you will need to stand up for yourself or for others. That is the sign of true assertion—a person who is able to act in accordance with his or her beliefs.

QUALITY FOUR: RESILIENCE

So the researcher says, "Heck no, we don't want fumbling under-graduates in our lab." Or your professor advises you to choose another career. Or your volunteer work at the hospital turns out not so great. Is that the end of you?

Of course not.

All of us encounter situations that eat away at our self-esteem. Instead of thinking, "Am I smart enough? Can I really make it?" ask yourself, "What must I do to carry on?" This is the voice of your pick-me-back-up mechanism.

Paradoxically, the pick-me-back-up mechanism is cultivated by failure. Each time you're down, you assess the situation. You gain some insight into yourself. And you emerge stronger, with a confidence that no matter what comes your way, you can deal with it.

QUALITY FIVE: FORESIGHT

You may find yourself in the library, eyes droopy over a physics book. And you may curse that fifteen-page term paper the week before it's due. Wouldn't you love to crawl into bed or to flee the library and join your friends? But you don't—not always. Why not? Because you know that these tasks, however unbearable at the time, are necessary to bring you closer to your long-term goal.

It's not about sacrifice as much as it is about foresight. Rather than having everything you want at one point in your life, you do it in steps. As Elena pointed out, "The average life expectancy for women in this country is more than eighty years. Compared to the early 1900s, when women used to die in their forties and fifties, that's almost two lifetimes." With foresight, you can delay gratification of immediate pleasures knowing that you are planning for an entire life.

8

A FRESH START
ON ACADEMICS

Regardless of who you were in high school—a teacher's pet or an embarrassment to the school—in college you begin again. If you were an all-around star in high school, college gives you a chance to apply your motivation in new directions. If you only did so-so in high school—wake up! It may be your time to shine. Many students who for various reasons didn't do well in high school find themselves to be top academic achievers in college.

Our advice on academics: start off full force. Once you get the ball moving, it's easier to keep up the momentum. Students who squander their first year spend the next three years trying to make up for past performance. Consider this: If you get a mixture of Cs and Bs in your first year (say, a grade point average of 2.5), you will need to get almost straight As in the next three years to bring your final cumulative GPA to a 3.5. This is like tying a lead weight around your ankle in the first leg of a relay race.

PLANNING YOUR
ACADEMIC PROGRAM

In order to graduate from college you must take courses in your major field of study as well as general education courses required for your degree (B.A. or B.S.). The pre-medical student must also complete medical school admissions requirements.

Most schools have more than one hundred different major areas of study. A major typically focuses on one academic discipline (history, economics, chemistry) but may be multidisciplinary (women's studies, Third World studies). Each major has core classes and electives.

General education requirements include courses in English, math, history, art, communication, the social sciences and basic sciences, physical education, and foreign languages. These requirements may be extensive and are different for each school and degree program.

The standard basic science work required for admission to most medical schools includes courses in biology, inorganic (general) chemistry, organic chemistry, and physics. Some schools have additional science requirements, such as vertebrate physiology or genetics. A year of college English and of calculus (with or without a semester of differential equations) are also required at most schools. *Medical School Admission Requirements* (MSAR), published annually by the Association of American Medical Colleges (AAMC), lists specific prerequisites for each school (see References and Suggested Readings for Chapter 11).

Create a Master Plan

Planning your academic schedule involves juggling these different requirements and completing them in a timely manner. Start by creating a master plan—the "to do" list of your academic years. Write down what you need to accomplish at your school for each of the following:

- Major requirements
- General requirements
- Medical school requirements

Establish a time line to complete this course work. Most full-time students complete a degree in four years. Students who need to take remedial course work in the sciences, or who are planning to take a double or a nonscience major, may need to spread the courses over five years or take more classes per semester or in the summer.

Fortunately, you don't have to plan all this on your own. Make an appointment with an academic advisor in your department or with the pre-medical advisor at your school. Meet with this person at least once a year to assess your progress.

Strategies for Pre-medical Students

To prepare successfully for medical school, the pre-medical student should focus on the following strategies.

TAKE APPROPRIATE SCIENCE CLASSES

There are usually three levels of difficulty for each basic science course. Pre-medical students should elect the middle-level courses, which provide a solid preparation for the Medical College Admissions Test (MCAT) and fulfill the requirements for most medical schools.

A handful of medical schools request that you enroll in the highest-level courses, the ones designed for students in that major. Unless you are planning to apply to one of these schools, we discourage this route. The highest-level courses are time-consuming. They include a lot of extra information and more math than are used on the MCAT or needed to prepare for medical school. The lowest-level courses (the general concepts courses) are not accepted by most medical schools.

Where you start with your science course work, and the pace at which you proceed, depends on your high school background and preparation. Students who have taken high school courses in the sciences and advanced math (precalculus or calculus) should be prepared to tackle college-level science courses immediately. If you do not feel confident about your math and science knowledge entering college, you should consult your academic advisor. Your advisor may discuss strategies to ensure your academic success: adjusting your schedule to take a lighter load, taking remedial course work in the sciences, or utilizing tutoring services to bring yourself up to speed.

Students often enroll in advanced science classes with the idea that this will help them either to get into medical school or to be more prepared once they get there. Not true. For example, if a medical school does not require classes in genetics or physiology, it means that they teach these classes later on the assumption that students have never seen the material before.

SEQUENCE COURSE WORK APPROPRIATELY

Planning course work with regard to sequence and timing will allow you to maximize learning and prepare yourself appropriately for the MCAT. You should complete all your basic science classes before you take the MCAT, usually by the end of your junior year (see

Chapter 9). To do this, you need to pace yourself. For an example of course sequencing, see the box below.

Suggested Undergraduate Science Course Sequencing
- Year 1: General Chemistry (with lab), General Biology (with lab), or Calculus
- Year 2: Organic Chemistry (with lab), General Biology (with lab), or Calculus
- Year 3: Physics

The courses listed in the box are usually offered in sequence, for instance, Math 205, Math 206, over several semesters. Whenever possible, take one course immediately after the next, and schedule the corresponding labs for the same time. This is even more important for course series that must be completed before you can advance to another course; for example, General Chemistry is a prerequisite for Organic Chemistry. If you fall behind in one course sequence, it may cause other scheduled course work to be delayed.

DEMONSTRATE A HIGH LEVEL OF ACADEMIC PERFORMANCE

Undergraduate GPA, particularly in the sciences, is one of the most important factors in admission to medical school. Not only that, but all the information you learn in the basic sciences will come back on the MCAT and will be the foundation for further learning in medical school. Students can best prepare themselves for medical school by learning this material well the first time.

Students should illustrate by their course work that they can handle a rigorous academic curriculum. Basic science course work should be completed at a four-year college or university rather than at a junior college or a community college. You should be enrolled in a reasonable number of classes each semester—four classes on average.

SCHEDULING CLASSES

Each semester you have a new selection of classes, professors, and class times. From this, you create your own schedule. There are a minimum number of classes you must take to be considered a full-time student and a maximum number for which you may formally register without special approval.

All students preregister for classes before the semester starts. Even so, you can rarely avoid the scheduling mayhem at the beginning of each semester. Students are attending classes they're formally enrolled in, trying to pick up classes they're not enrolled in, and standing in long lines to add, drop, and change grading options.

To get the best classes and teachers with the minimum amount of effort, follow these rules.

LOOK BEFORE YOU LEAP
Don't trust the course catalog when registering for classes. What seems to be an interactive class on the racial dynamics of urban planning may turn out to be a series of droned-out lectures. If you really want to find out what you're getting into, talk with other students before you enroll.

Ask the upperclassmen who the best lecturers are, whether they are supportive of students and easily accessible. While one professor may hold a coffee hour with students after a lecture, another skips off to her research lab and is nowhere to be found.

GET THE TEACHING JEWELS
Don't miss the professor who simulates geometric molecular shapes with his body—even if it's an 8 A.M. class. Better to be a little groggy with an enthusiastic teacher than to be wide awake for a lifeless one. Beware of the "weed out" professors (every university has a few), the ones with a propensity for failing half the class on exams.

ONLY TAKE WHAT YOU CAN HANDLE
You don't need to impress medical schools with academic masochism. Overloading yourself with advanced-level classes only ensures that you'll be a stressed-out wreck and compromises your learning and grades. Take into consideration the difficulty of a class and the time commitment. If you have to take a five-credit advanced calculus class, balance it with a few lighter, less demanding courses.

KEEP A DIVERSE SCHEDULE
Even the most fascinating material becomes monotonous if it's the only thing you ever do. Try spending eight hours a day, five days a

week, pondering molecules you can't see. No matter how fervently you love chemistry, the material loses some of its sparkle.

Perk up your schedule with one or two general education courses each semester. When you're burnt out on quantum mechanics, you can relax with a short story by Ama Ata Aidoo. You may find one class so enthralling that you decide to pursue a minor (usually eight to ten courses) in that subject area or even to change your major. More than 30 percent of all students graduate with a different major than the one they started with in freshman year.

Grading Options

If you are interested in a class but don't want to be preoccupied with your grade, consider auditing the class or taking it pass/no pass. Usually there's a limit on the number of pass/no pass courses that can count toward your major. All the courses required for admission to medical school should be taken for a letter grade.

Adding and Dropping Classes

For the first few weeks, you can add and drop classes. Consider this a trial run. You get an idea of how interesting and difficult the classes will be, and you have the chance to adjust your schedule.

Dropping a class is easy. It's adding one that is tricky, especially if the class or professor is popular. Once a class fills to maximum capacity, it is officially closed, which means that you need permission from the professor to enroll. On the first day of class, there is a waiting list that's passed around. As people drop out over the first couple of weeks, the professor will sign others in. To make sure you're at the top of the list, you should attend every lecture, sit in the front row, and be persistent with the professor (without getting too annoying).

Some students avoid the hassle of adding by enrolling in more classes than they plan to take, then dropping the ones they don't want. At some schools, you can even register for the same course with different professors. This strategy will get you better classes and teachers if you have the endurance to sit through multiple lectures and different sections of the same class at the start of each semester.

Withdrawing from a Class

After a certain period of time, you cannot drop a class. Instead you withdraw and receive a W on your record. Many students get their first grey hair deciding whether to withdraw after a grade of 42 percent on the first chemistry lab report or to continue and possibly get a bad grade for the entire course.

What's worse on your transcript—a W or a bad grade? Certainly a W is preferable to a failing grade, especially in a core science class. However, serious discretion is advised in withdrawing, since medical schools do not overlook these blemishes. Recent studies indicate that a significant number of withdrawals or incompletes in undergraduate course work predicts academic difficulty in medical school. This stands to reason: in medical school all students have to progress at the same pace; withdrawing from a course is not an option.

Thus, a general rule: one or two withdrawals, okay. But try to avoid them if you can. Take measures to enroll yourself in classes that suit you. If you find yourself in academic trouble, see what you can do to remedy the problem.

STUDYING STRATEGIES

Good students know that it's not how much you study but your approach to studying that makes the difference.

STUDY TO LEARN
Most of the time, your learning coincides with your performance on tests and papers, but not always. Sometimes you'll scoot by with a grade you don't deserve, and sometimes you'll learn more than could ever be reflected on an exam. Each of us needs an internal and independent standard by which to evaluate our efforts.

FOLLOW YOUR OWN RHYTHM
How, where, when, even how long to study are different for every person. Some people can read for hours and retain every word. Others need to hear information out loud. Some of us are at our prime at 3 A.M. Others concentrate best in the morning. There is no "right" way to study, like outlining chapters in the library with your face to the

wall (as one book instructs). The best approach is what works for you. Experiment with different study techniques: flash cards, outlines, or study groups. Use your natural circadian rhythms to get the most out of your study time. Study in a place where you feel comfortable and that is free from distractions.

DEVELOP A STUDY STRATEGY FOR EACH COURSE
Each class will have different time commitments and responsibilities, and may require a different approach to learning. Your memorization skills may get you through chemistry, but they won't help you to learn poetry. Doing problem sets with friends may be helpful for physics but a waste of time for biology.

What's more, every professor has his or her own way of teaching a course, with different expectations of students. Testing material may come from lecture or the assigned textbook. Certain professors want you to understand and be able to apply concepts; others expect you to regurgitate the graph on page 248 of the text.

MAXIMIZE YOUR STUDY TIME
A few mental tricks will help you learn more efficiently and retain what you learn. First, concentrate on making the material you study more interesting. Research shows that you more easily remember interesting material. If your mind is not that easily fooled—if you can't learn to love memorizing organic chemistry reactions—resort to other methods. Talk it over with friends; use colored pens; draw pictures.

Second, break your study time into intervals. Read for short periods (around ten minutes), then quickly review what you have just read. Researchers believe that this study-relax-review-continue method causes the material to be merged into long-term memory storage (like moving information from RAM to a hard drive) by firing up an area of the brain called the dentate gyrus. It also takes advantage of the fact that people remember the first and the last part of what they have read better than the middle part.

For suggestions on improving your note-taking methods, see the box on the next page.

Third, use different approaches to learn the same material. What you don't pick up from lecture, you may understand by reading the textbook. Rather than read your lecture notes another time, try teach-

Note Taking

Everyone has a special way of taking notes. Some students use twenty different colored pens and make elaborate notes, while others scrawl notes in outline form down the center of the page. If you wish to improve your note taking, consider the method recommended by experts.

Use the right-hand side of the page for taking the notes. After the lecture, review the material and make additional notes in the left-hand margin (see illustration). While it is best to do this immediately after a lecture, taking a break will probably be more urgent, but set aside a certain amount of time when you get home for reviewing and adding to the notes.

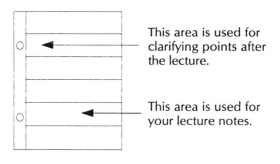

This area is used for clarifying points after the lecture.

This area is used for your lecture notes.

ing them to someone else. Don't rely on repetition (unless you only want to memorize).

Read the course syllabus carefully before you throw it into your file crate. It explains the structure of the course and the breakdown of points for assignments and exams. Consider visiting the professor during office hours in the first week of each course. Ask for advice on how to study for the course and on other resources that may be of assistance to you.

TAKE ADVANTAGE OF ACADEMIC SUPPORT SERVICES

The university abounds with teachers. Your professors are available during office hours. Teaching assistants (usually graduate students in the department) often conduct weekly discussion groups and review sessions. Many schools also have tutoring centers. Most students know about these services, but few actually use them.

THINK OF THIS AS EXTRA TEACHING
Instead of struggling over your physics homework, review the questions with a tutor. Make an appointment with the professor a few days before your biology exam to discuss the things you have learned.

Getting input from others, whether your professor, your best friend, or a tutor, makes the learning process easier. Another person may give you a new angle from which to understand the material or correct the things that you have misunderstood. They may give you tips on better, more efficient ways to study the material.

ASSESSING YOUR ACADEMIC SITUATION

It helps to periodically evaluate your progress in each course. Keep track of your grades in a separate notebook. That way you always know exactly your academic status and what you need to do to accomplish your goals.

Identifying Areas of Difficulty

If you are having academic trouble, try to identify the cause.

ACADEMIC PREPARATION
Ask yourself, Do I have the background to do well in this class? What are my areas of deficiency?

Students often dive headfirst into difficult classes or a heavy load of classes with unrealistic expectations. If you're having difficulty in a class, you may need to step back and ask whether you are academically prepared to handle all that you have taken on.

This is particularly important for new students. A student with minimal high school science preparation begins college at a different level than someone who has taken advanced-level courses. In addition, because we are each unique individuals, we have different abilities. It's necessary to recognize your background and abilities so that you can take the necessary steps to achieve. You can still get an A in that chemistry class, but it may mean you need to take other classes first or get extra tutoring or simply put in more effort.

Remember, it's achievement that matters. If you're too embarrassed or too proud to admit that you're in over your head, you'll go down silently. Better to be honest with yourself now than to suffer later.

STUDY HABITS

Studying for an eight-hour spurt before the exam doesn't suffice most of the time. Similarly, you shouldn't be surprised if you don't do well one semester when you barely crack a book. Poor effort begets poor performance.

Then again, maybe you're putting in the time and effort but you aren't doing as well as you would hope. You may have the potential but aren't maximizing your learning.

Look at how, when, and how long you study, with a critical eye to efficiency. You may enjoy studying with friends, but if it takes you ten hours to get anything accomplished, it's not a good use of your time. Similarly, you may feel responsible for attending a lecture when you're very tired, but if you spend the hour snoozing, you're better off skipping it or figuring out how to become a more active participant in the lecture hour.

For tips on how to make the best use of lectures and study time, review the previous section on studying.

TEST-TAKING SKILLS

Nothing is more frustrating than studying for a class, knowing that you know the material, but not being able to demonstrate this on an exam. If this is a common scenario for you, you need to examine your test-taking skills.

For many students, it's anxiety that poses a problem. These students need to focus on strategies to relieve the anxiety associated with the testing process—taking a practice exam or spending a few minutes before the exam clearing their minds. If you find that you run out of time, you need to pace yourself. Others have the opposite problem; they rush through and make careless mistakes. These students need to take more time, read the questions more carefully, and double-check their answers.

Getting Help

The first person you should see when you are having academic difficulty in a course is your professor. He or she may help you to assess your problem areas and find a solution. If you do poorly on an exam, go over the questions that you got wrong with the professor. Find out whether it's simply a matter of test-taking skills or whether you have a problem understanding the material. Ask for suggestions on how to improve your weak areas.

If you are considering dropping the class, explain this to the professor. Refrain from simply whining about grades, as many professors get irked at pre-medical students for this reason. Emphasize that you are concerned with both your marks and learning the material. There may be alternatives: the professor may allow you to retake the exam, do an extra project, or put more weight on another assignment/ exam for the class.

If you don't find the professor very receptive, you may wish to speak with an academic advisor or another professor whom you trust. You may also consider talking with a counselor on campus. Perhaps other factors in your life are interfering with your ability to perform in school. This person may refer you for further help with study methods, concentration, coping mechanisms, or time management.

TEACHERS, ADVOCATES, AND MENTORS

I remember the day I dissected the thorax in medical school. I was searching frantically for the subclavian vein—cutting and pulling— and had been for over an hour. It wasn't until I felt the hand of my professor on my shoulder and her voice, "Jennifer, step down. You've lost your perspective," that I withdrew from my frenzy. From that moment she became more than a teacher; she was a mentor. She would take me aside when I got nervous during an exam, talk to me about my plans for the future, and encourage my dreams. When she died last year, I recalled the lesson she taught me that day in the lab. I thought of how many times she had helped me to regain my perspective, not just in terms of anatomy, but in terms of my life.

We all need encouragement, someone to occasionally shake our perspective on the world or to make sure that we don't quit when things get tough. This is what we talked about in the last chapter when we emphasized community, what Facika describes as "people who are rooting for you." In the academic world, these people can be your professors.

There are two approaches that you as a student can have toward your professors. You can see them as evaluators—seek their approval, try to squeeze out a good grade, and grumble at their failings. Or—and this is what we recommend—you can approach them as people. Remember that people tend to react to you as you treat them. If you see them as your allies, ask for help, look to them for advice, you are likely to bring out the best in them.

Almost everyone we know will point to people who have helped them along the way. Remember, it was the encouragement of James's advisor after he got an A in Organic Chemistry that made him consider a career in the life sciences. Facika went back to her professors at her college when she needed help getting recommendations for medical school. Elena looked up to her grandmother, who was a journalist, a pediatrician, and a novelist, as an example of the many different things she could do with her life.

So where do you find those special people who will guide, support, and inspire you? Some of us stumble upon them by chance. Most of us, however, have to make a sustained effort. The most obvious place to approach your professors is in their offices during office hours. You may have a question regarding the material in class. If not, just go to talk—about your plans, your interests, your concerns. Ask for their feedback. Most professors feel flattered when someone genuinely asks them for advice rather than just coming in to argue about a grade.

You should take advantage of opportunities where you can work one-to-one with a professor. One way you may do this is to ask a professor to sponsor an independent study project. Other students seek research experiences.

Professors also get involved with student organizations or community service projects. By doing such work you have the opportunity to get to know your professors outside of the formal student-teacher relationship.

PART THREE

ENTERING MEDICAL SCHOOL

9

THE MEDICAL COLLEGE ADMISSIONS TEST (MCAT)

The Medical College Admissions Test (MCAT) has become a rite of passage for people who wish to apply to medical school. Over 70,000 MCATs are administered to aspiring medical school applicants each year.

To some pre-medical students, the MCAT is part of the routine—another challenge to be met on the way to a career in medicine. To others, it stands as a forbidding obstacle. As one pre-medical explains, "You can never really relax because you know you have to confront the MCAT. It is like a nasty troll waiting to trip you up as you cross the last bridge to medical school."

To almost all students, it is a source of some anxiety. Much of this anxiety fades once you remove the mystique of the MCAT to see it as it is—just another exam. As with most other exams, your performance is linked to your preparation, not your I.Q. or your luck. The person who does well is the one who puts forth time, effort, and thoughtful planning in the undergraduate years and in the months preceding the exam.

EVERYTHING YOU WANT TO KNOW ABOUT THE MCAT

If you are like many students, you are probably uncertain about what the MCAT is and what to expect of the exam. Here, we answer some of the most common questions students have.

What Is the MCAT?

The MCAT is a standardized exam administered to students who plan to apply to medical school after having completed basic pre-medical course work. The MCAT, developed by the Association of American Medical Colleges (AAMC), is one way that medical schools can determine if an applicant is academically prepared for medical school. The current exam emphasizes material in the sciences, but it is not solely a science knowledge exam.

What If I Don't Do Well on Standardized Exams?

Students who didn't do well on a standardized test like the Scholastic Aptitude Test (SAT) are sometimes terrified by the thought of having to take another one. But the MCAT, unlike the SAT, has no aptitude component. It is a measure of achievement, designed to test what you have learned in the undergraduate years.

If you have excelled in your undergraduate work, you have every reason to be confident about the MCAT, but that's only half the battle. Studying for the exam itself will make a difference, particularly if you are one of those people who has difficulty with standardized exams. Very few people, no matter how brilliant, can pull off the MCAT with little or no preparation beforehand.

What Is the Purpose of the MCAT?

Originally, the MCAT was designed to address high attrition rates in medical school. Performance above a baseline score (for example, a score of 10 or more) in the basic sciences indicated that an applicant was prepared for the academic rigors of medical school. Over time, the MCAT took on a subtle new role, from being an approximate indicator of academic competence to serving as a tool for distinguishing fine differences in academic ability among applicants.

Today, the majority of medical schools use the MCAT in the admissions process to select for the most highly qualified applicants. For example, an applicant with a subtest score of 12 would be considered more favorably than one with a score of 11. Only 14 percent of all schools use the MCAT as it was originally intended—to determine if an applicant meets minimum academic standards. These schools consider all MCAT scores above a certain cutoff point to be equal.

What Was the Controversy About the MCAT?

The expanded use of the MCAT in the medical school admissions process and its impact on pre-medical education have been the subject of some debate in the past decade. To many medical schools, the MCAT has unrivaled value—it is standardized. It tests the same information for all students at all schools. Admissions officials claim it is the great equalizer, the only objective means of evaluating the academic ability of students who come from more than three thousand different undergraduate institutions.

Most admissions practices are based on the premise that MCAT scores are a predictor of success. Research backing this claim shows a link between MCAT performance and success in the first two years of a medical school curriculum—the basic science years. A positive correlation between performance on the MCAT and Part 1 of the National Medical Boards Exam also is demonstrated. And yet, research shows little correlation between performance on the MCAT and success in the clinical years of medical school (the final two years) or beyond.

Furthermore, some medical educators argue that any benefit of using the MCAT in the admissions process is outweighed by its negative effect on pre-medical education. Called "the tail that wags the dog," the MCAT has been said to contribute to the problems that plague pre-medical education: overspecialization in the sciences, a focus on test knowledge rather than on the process of learning, and a preoccupation with grades. Former Harvard University President Derek Bok, in his opposition to the MCAT in its prior form, asserted that the MCAT and other science-focused admissions requirements "convey the misleading message that medicine, at bottom, is simply a matter of applying scientific knowledge."

Controversy about the MCAT, coinciding with other trends in medical school admissions practices, led to its overhaul in 1991. The new MCAT is designed to be more relevant to current medical school curricula and clinical practice. It includes material in the humanities and social sciences, and tests skills in problem solving and critical thinking. Verbal reasoning is now one-third of the exam—medical schools consider it the second most important MCAT subtest. Another change is the addition of a writing sample—two essays that may also be used to supplement the admissions process (medical schools may request to see the essays).

These changes in the MCAT convey the message that the best pre-medical preparation is a well-rounded education. Students are encouraged to use the undergraduate years to explore areas outside science; to read books in literature and history; and to learn to analyze, interpret, and communicate.

What Does the New MCAT Look Like?

The new MCAT is designed to be less burdensome to test-takers. It is eighty minutes shorter than the old exam and emphasizes conceptual understanding rather than rote science recall. It also has fewer science and quantitative tests and fewer discrete knowledge (independent factual knowledge) questions.

The new MCAT is condensed into four subtests: the physical sciences, the biological sciences, verbal reasoning, and a writing sample. Total testing time is 5 3/4 hours.

I. PHYSICAL SCIENCES (77 questions, 100 minutes)

The physical sciences section covers concepts in physics and general chemistry. It consists of ten or eleven sets of questions. Each set of questions is preceded by textual information that may include graphs, experiments, and illustrations. To answer the questions, you must analyze the information and apply knowledge of certain principles and concepts. Basic mathematical skills up to calculus are necessary. For example, you may be asked to use your knowledge of solution chemistry to interpret experimental results and respond to questions on boiling points or precipitates.

There are also fifteen discrete knowledge questions in this section. For example, a question may give the wavelength and speed of a sound wave and ask you to calculate its velocity. (Recall that velocity = speed x wavelength).

II. BIOLOGICAL SCIENCES (77 questions, 100 minutes)

The biological sciences section covers concepts in biology and organic chemistry. There are approximately four to eight passages followed by questions on the material. The questions test your ability to integrate your knowledge of basic biological concepts with the information provided to solve problems. For example, you may be asked to use your knowledge of intracellular parasitic life cycles and the concept of selection to answer questions on a passage about rickettsias.

As with the physical sciences section, there are fifteen discrete knowledge questions not associated with a reading passage. For example, you may be asked to select the correct geometric structure of an amino acid at its isoelectric point.

III. VERBAL REASONING (65 questions, 85 minutes)

The verbal reasoning section contains texts in prose form on topics in the humanities, social, and natural sciences. The passages are 500–600 words long, followed by 6 to 10 multiple choice questions. These questions are designed to test reading comprehension, reasoning ability, and critical thinking. For example, you may read a passage about Voltaire and be asked to interpret the meaning of statements contained in the passage.

IV. WRITING SAMPLE (2 questions, 30 minutes each)

This section includes two essays in which you respond to a statement or quote, for example, "No matter how oppressive a government, violent revolution is never justified." Your tasks are several: explain briefly what the statement means, discuss opposing sides of the issue, and provide examples supporting your position.

The writing sample is designed to assess basic writing skills rather than personal beliefs. You should establish a central theme or thesis, supply justification for your position, and formulate a conclusion. You will be evaluated on your ability to present ideas clearly and to follow proper grammar and syntax rules.

How Are MCAT Scores Determined?

The scores on the multiple choice sections are determined by converting your raw score—the total number you answer correctly (no penalty for incorrect answers)—to a scaled score that ranges from 1 to 15.

The scaled score takes into account the level of difficulty of the questions. That way, if one edition of the MCAT is more or less difficult than another, a score of 9 still represents the same level of academic ability in the test-taker. Reducing the scale also prevents admissions committees from comparing candidates based on minute differences in scores that may be due to other factors, such as good guessing skills.

The writing section is graded by a different scale. Each essay is given a score from 1 to 6 by two different readers. The total score for the writing sample is the sum of these four scores (two essays times two readers), which is then converted to an alphabetical score ranging from J (lowest) to T (highest). These letters were selected to escape the loaded meanings of the traditional A–F letter scores.

When Will I Receive My Scores?

Approximately four to six weeks after you take the MCAT, you will receive your scores, one for each of the three multiple choice subtests (physical sciences, biological sciences, and verbal reasoning) and the writing section.

How Are MCAT Scores Sent to Schools?

By signing a release statement on your MCAT registration, you give permission for your scores to be automatically forwarded to all partic- ipating AMCAS (American Medical College Application Service) schools to which you apply. In addition, you may forward your scores to as many as six non-AMCAS schools, including AACOMAS (American Association of Colleges of Osteopathic Medicine Applica- tion Services). You will have the opportunity to list these schools on the test day, so you should know by the day of the exam where you want to apply (see Chapter 10, Choosing a Medical School). Any additional colleges or choices after the test date require additional fees.

How Do Admissions Committees Use the Scores?

Most schools examine MCAT scores in the initial screening of appli- cants, though each school has its own policy for how the MCAT is used and its weight relative to other factors (see Chapter 11, The Application Process). Usually, MCAT scores are considered one of the most important factors in medical school admission, along with undergraduate GPA, letters of recommendation, and state residence. However, a handful of schools, including Johns Hopkins, do not require the MCAT at all.

It is common for schools to place more emphasis on the MCAT for applicants from less competitive or unknown schools, or where the grading system is different from the standard A–F system (for example, some schools use written evaluations). Under these circumstances, the MCAT may be the primary criterion to determine an applicant's academic qualifications.

What If MCAT Scores and GPA Don't Match?

Some students see the MCAT as a second chance, a way to compensate for poor performance in the undergraduate years. Often, this is true, particularly if it is only a matter of poor grades in a few classes or in your early undergraduate years. High MCAT scores, however, are not going to resurrect you from the dead if you have goofed off for four years.

Good students rarely mess up on the day of the exam, although that seems to be a common fear. If you have a respectable GPA from a well-known undergraduate institution and good letters of recommendation, less-than-stellar MCAT scores will not ruin you. If there is a large discrepancy, the committee will take a closer look at your academic record or seek further evaluation, perhaps through the interview, to figure out what is going on.

When Should I Take the MCAT?

Applicants typically take the MCAT in the year that they apply to medical school, that is, approximately eighteen months before they will enter medical school.

The MCAT is administered in the spring (April) and summer (August) of each year. The spring exam is preferable. Medical schools usually will not review an application until it is complete with MCAT scores. Taking the spring exam puts you in the first wave of applications and leaves you more time to manage all the other details associated with applying to medical school. It also leaves the summer date as a backup, in the event that you need to retake the exam. You can take the exam once in April and once in August of each year only (no makeup exams).

In practice, however, many people wait until the summer exam. This allows you more time to prepare or to finish course work. The obvious drawback is that your primary or AMCAS application will not begin to be processed until the MCAT results arrive. This could be as late as October or November. By that time, other applicants are completing secondary applications and even interviewing at schools. This puts you at a disadvantage in the admissions process and brings you to the wire with application deadlines.

When Do I Register for the MCAT?

You should register for the MCAT at least a month in advance. Late registration (up to two weeks before the exam) requires an additional late fee. MCAT registration packets are available in early February for the year in which you are taking the exam.

A registration packet with up-to-date deadlines can be obtained by writing or calling:

MCAT Program Office
P.O. Box 4056
Iowa City, IA 52243-4056
(319) 337-1357 (M–F 8:30 A.M.–4:30 P.M., Central Time)

The registration packet includes information about the MCAT, some sample test items, registration materials, a fee reduction program application, and an order form for publications related to the MCAT. There is also an order form for Association of American Medical Colleges (AAMC) publications related to the MCAT.

The regular examination fee is $155. People with extreme financial limitations may apply for a fee waiver through the MCAT Fee Reduction Program. The application for this waiver must be submitted approximately six weeks in advance of the exam.

PREPARING FOR THE MCAT

The MCAT—like it or not—is one of the "must-do"s of the premedical years. Preparation should begin the day you arrive at college (or when you decide you want to go to medical school).

Planning Your Undergraduate Course Work

During your undergraduate years, you should take a year each of general biology, inorganic and organic chemistry, and physics. A course in biochemistry, although not required, may be helpful. A year of calculus, English, and courses in the social sciences and humanities are also helpful.

Introductory-level courses in the sciences are appropriate (and recommended) to prepare for the MCAT. If you are gung-ho about an advanced-level chemistry class, take it for interest, not because it will give you an edge on the MCAT. In fact, studies show that non-science majors taking the minimum science prerequisites have scores on the MCAT comparable to those of science majors. In Chapter 8, we mentioned other suggestions for planning your undergraduate curriculum.

Don't take the exam until you have finished appropriate course work, preferably right afterward, while the material is fresh in your mind. If you have difficulty in a certain subject, you should work on this well before the MCAT approaches. Some students get tutoring. Others tutor the material themselves once they get a better grip on it. Teaching a subject gives you a deeper understanding of the material and is good preparation for the MCAT.

Adapting to the Demands of the MCAT

The MCAT is different from some other exams to which you have become accustomed. First, it is long. Despite the recent reduction in MCAT examination time, you can expect to be at the testing site for most of the day—from 8 A.M. till 5:30 P.M. (this includes two ten-minute breaks and a one-hour lunch). Second, it is standardized. This means strict rules, time limitations, and more bubble-in forms than you will ever care to see. The testing conditions can be, not surprisingly, overbearing and tense. Test-takers shuffle nervously to rooms by alphabetical order (with special rooms for left-handed people). Identification and test passes (including fingerprints) are checked at the door. The exams are passed out, collected, and checked with militarylike precision and order.

To adapt to the demands of the MCAT, you need to develop a few special skills. The first is endurance, both mental and physical. Try to remember how you feel after a three-hour final, and multiply this by three. In order to keep up your oomph throughout the day, you need to condition yourself. Take a few full-length practice exams in the weeks before the actual exam to develop your concentration. Build physical endurance by keeping a healthy lifestyle—eat well and get enough sleep.

The second skill is familiarization. As you study for the MCAT, you should become familiar with the format of the exam, the types of questions, and the testing procedures. The more familiar you are with the format and testing process, the more prepared you will be to take the exam.

The next skill is desensitization. Mentally anticipate and desensitize yourself from anxiety surrounding the testing day and its conditions. Know how you function under time pressure. If you find other people's stress to be contagious, avoid the nervous nellies.

Consider rehearsing the day of the exam. Get up one Saturday and drive out to the exam site at the time you will arrive for the actual exam. Find the parking lot, walk around, look for a place to have lunch and relax. It may sound silly, but not worrying about getting lost and knowing your way around the test site will take the edge off anxiety on the day of the MCAT.

Building Confidence for the MCAT

Studies show that if you believe in yourself, you can accomplish more. The term for this is *self-efficacy,* the belief that you can pursue and attain goals, such as a certain career.

Self-efficacy also affects exam performance. Fair enough, you say, but how do you develop a cool and confident perspective on your MCAT-taking ability?

First, you must overcome your fears. Define what it is that makes you nervous about the MCAT. Perhaps the amount of material intimidates you. Or you bombed physics. Or you are haunted by a bad experience with the SAT.

Determine whether these fears are realistic. After talking with others, you may find that the MCAT is not nearly as grueling as you had previously expected. You may find, after reviewing your physics book, that you are not as hopelessly lost as you first thought.

Convert your fears into markers for areas that need improvement. In other words, transform your fears into something productive. If you have problems with standardized exams, you can work on your test-taking skills. Many colleges offer courses or workshops in this or related areas such as stress management. If a certain subject causes anxiety, concentrate your study efforts to strengthen this area. As you confront and overcome these vulnerabilities, your self-confidence will grow.

Studying for the MCAT

The amount of material covered by the MCAT at first glance seems overwhelming. Your first reaction is, How can I learn all of it?

The fact is, you've already learned the material. Studying for the MCAT is review. Don't panic if you cannot remember the geometric shape of cyanide off the top of your head. The concept of orbital electron pairs and electronegativity has probably settled in the recesses of your mind. Be assured that it is still there.

A few components are needed to put those rusty wheels into motion: motivation, time, and work. We know that you've been working hard for the past few years, so we don't want you to fizzle out in the final stretch. Here are some ways that will help you keep the momentum going on the MCAT.

MOTIVATION

Ask the average pre-medical student what he or she thinks of the MCAT and you'll get a groan. It is seen as a nuisance and a waste of time. It's no wonder that motivation isn't surging when it comes to cracking that big MCAT review book. "I'll start next weekend" you say to yourself every week, until you realize it's now or never.

Most of us begrudge doing things that are forced on us from the outside and that are not enjoyable.

So let's look at the MCAT another way. Psychologists call this technique cognitive restructuring. Think of how studying for the MCAT will *benefit* you. Weren't there times that something piqued your interest, but then it was, "quick, on to the next topic"? Now you have the time to figure out how that particularly baffling cross of green and blue bugs came out with speckled offspring.

If all else fails, think about how badly you want to be a doctor. Ultimately, if you have decided that you really want to pursue a future in medicine, then studying for this exam will help you get there.

Even so, occasionally you will get the MCAT blues. Who wants to spend eight hours every Saturday in the library breathing book dust and photocopier fumes?

The following tips will help you keep motivated (save these — you'll need them in medical school):

- Take note of what you accomplish as you study. Even if you learn the information on only ten pages, it's more than you knew before. Never look ahead when you are discouraged; look back and see how far you have come.
- Study in a way that makes you happy. If you hate libraries, don't force yourself to go to one. Study in a cafe or a quiet spot outside.
- Personalize the study process. Be creative with your study techniques. Make a collage of your notes, create an index card collection, give yourself weekly quizzes.
- Reward yourself. Tell yourself that if you study a certain amount, you'll go out dancing with friends, or spend time with family, or eat at your favorite restaurant. Stick a gold star on your forehead—whatever makes you feel good.
- Visualize success. Remember self-efficacy? Think of yourself tackling the exam comfortably, finishing in plenty of time, and tossing your books in the trash (or gladly bequeathing them to a friend).

FINDING TIME TO STUDY

You may ask, Where will I find the time to study? The answer is that you already have time. It's just a matter of how you use it.

This is called time management. It's really person management, and the person is you. The following may help:

- Write down what you need to accomplish for the MCAT and establish a time line for these tasks. Some people study in little bites over a period of six months, others go the intensive route for six weeks. Do what has worked for you in the past. Just be realistic. You cannot memorize your organic chemistry text over a long weekend. Remember to schedule more time for the difficult subjects.
- Make adjustments in your life. Most students already have a full schedule. Something has to give—less time working on the campus newspaper or a lighter course schedule. Otherwise, it's your sanity that will suffer.
- Set aside a particular number of hours per week to study. Protect this time from intrusion. Turn off the ringer on the telephone. If friends tend to stop by, go somewhere else.

• Assess your progress. If you fall behind in one subject, you may need to give your schedule a face-lift—pick up the pace, put in more hours, or change the way you study. As long as you adjust your schedule early on, you won't find yourself a week before the exam underprepared.

DEVISING A WORK PLAN

You can't attack the MCAT in a haphazard fashion. You need to take an organized approach to the tasks and material that await you. Here's our advice:

• Know the major subjects and concepts that the MCAT covers. Use the MCAT Student Manual for this. Go over an old exam to get an idea of the depth to which it covers the material and the level of difficulty of the problems. Use this information to direct your studying.

• Review the content matter. The best way to do this is to invest in one of the many commercial MCAT study guides (see References and Suggested Readings at the end of this book). Many of the MCAT courses also provide study materials. These books review the material at a level and depth that is appropriate for the MCAT.

   You may wish to refer to lecture notes or college texts to clarify material, but not as the primary source. Lecture notes tend to be incomplete and may not correlate with the material that the MCAT covers. Beware of the college text unless you're interested in swallowing down masses of detail.

   Some people recommend that you begin with your easiest subject, to build up confidence. This is good advice as long as you do not spend all your time polishing your strengths and ignore your weak areas until the last minute. Perhaps the thought of physics vectors throws you into a panic. But if you don't confront this weakness and work to improve yourself, you'll be stuck on the day of the exam exactly where you left off—not knowing the material (and more anxious than ever).

   After you have reviewed the material, answer the workbook questions and take mini-exams. Be careful not to take these exams prematurely. If you are not ready, then doing test questions will be a source of discouragement rather than learning.

   The workbook exercises will help you identify your strengths and weaknesses. Instead of simply acknowledging what you did right, focus on the questions that you got wrong. If you don't understand why a certain answer is incorrect, ask someone to explain it to you. Remember, similar questions will appear on the exam.

- In the last stage of your preparation, take at least one full-length practice exam. Replicate the conditions of the testing day—use timers, bubble sheets, a sixty-minute lunch—everything. (And no calculators!)

  Evaluate yourself immediately after taking the practice MCAT. What was the most challenging aspect of the exam? Did you lose time on certain tests? What errors did you make? You may discover even the little things that affect your performance, like being tired in the afternoon because you ate too much at lunch.

  Spend the last few weeks improving your weakest areas: studying more on one subject, pacing yourself better, or double-checking your math.

- Gather your peace before the exam. Some people spend an hour alone or meditate on the day of the exam. Anita found it helpful to get her mind off the exam: "I had a great breakfast with a friend of mine. For an hour we had this nostalgic conversation about gymnastics. We didn't talk about the MCAT at all."

Should I Take an MCAT Preparation Course?

Many students enroll in commercial MCAT courses. The courses typically last eight weeks. The basic regimen of these courses—reviewing material, developing test-taking skills, and familiarizing yourself with the exam—can be done on your own.

What these courses do is save you the hassle of preparing by yourself. They give you review books and testing materials. They force you to stay on schedule and to structure your study time. Some people find it easier to stay motivated when surrounded by other people with a similar focus.

For people who need a lot of work, the MCAT tutorial centers offer a virtually unlimited supply of practice exams and workbooks with tutorials. Some students, however, have complained that the exercises and tests at these centers are not at the same level of difficulty as the actual MCAT. If they're too hard, you become distraught that you don't know anything. If they're too easy, you gain false confidence and may be underprepared for the exam.

Before you empty your savings or take out an additional loan to pay for one of these courses (they can run up to $800), talk with others who have taken the course and the MCAT. Some courses offer a fee waiver (about 25–30 percent) for people with financial limitations. If self-motivation is one of your strengths, you may decide that there are better ways to spend your money. Fifty dollars buys you a good MCAT review text.

10

CHOOSING A MEDICAL SCHOOL

with Peter Muennig, M.D.

Contrary to popular belief, all medical schools are not the same. Medical schools differ almost as much as undergraduate institutions: in educational philosophy, academic curriculum, makeup of the faculty and students, type of facilities, and other aspects.

Students often focus exclusively on what they must do to be accepted to medical school and overlook the *choosing* of a medical school. It's no wonder this is the case. Both the pre-medical environment and the application process are extremely competitive. Most pre-medical students think they don't have a choice. In reality, if you have reasonable academic qualifications, you will have several options. By applying to schools that are compatible with your personal values and career goals, you will have even more. The admissions process at each school favors students who fit with the school's mission, whether they be students interested in primary care and innovative learning or aspiring neurosurgeons.

Your choice of a medical school will be one of the most critical decisions of your career and your life. Take the time to examine your options in medical education. Think about where you will fit in—the school that will challenge you most, maximize your learning, and utilize your talents. This is where you have the greatest chance for success and ultimately happiness.

As Facika notes,

It was important to me to be practical and realistic when choosing a medical school. Then, too, I responded to a gut feeling about where I would belong. So I looked at the quality of the education, the general atmosphere of the school, the diversity of the students, and the cost. All those factors came together for me in my choice of a medical school.

WHAT DO YOU KNOW ABOUT MEDICAL EDUCATION?

You may have taken undergraduate classes in anatomy, worked in a hospital, or had other experiences that convince you that you want to be a physician. Yet there is still a lot you probably don't know about the four or more years of your life when you will be training for the medical profession. For example, what are the characteristics that make a medical school unique? What are the different approaches to teaching medicine? What resources and opportunities are available to you as a medical student?

The questionnaire on the next several pages will introduce you to some of your options in medical training and give you an idea of the characteristics of a medical school that may particularly appeal to you.

EXAMINE YOUR PRIORITIES FOR MEDICAL SCHOOL

As you note in the questionnaire, many factors will affect your education and your life as a medical student. Let's examine these issues in more depth.

Prestige

Students often place high priority on a school's academic reputation. But does the reputation of a school correspond to the quality of the medical education at that school? Not necessarily. In fact, some rankings of medical schools—if you read them carefully—rate criteria such as library holdings equal to teaching quality. Unless the number of scientific journals in the library is at the top of your priority list,

Evaluating a Medical School According to Your Needs

	Most Important	Least Important	Not Sure

Prestige

1. How important is it that the school have a prestigious name? — ✓ (Not Sure)

2. How important is the reputation of the faculty? — ✓ (Not Sure)

Pre-Clinical Education

3. How important is it that your pre-clinical education be one of the following?

   a. A traditional basic sciences program

   b. An organ systems approach

   c. A case-based learning method

4. What learning modality do you prefer?

   a. Lecture

   b. Small group — ✓ (Most Important)

   c. Independent study — ✓ (Not Sure)

5. Is it important for you to be taught by

   a. Clinicians? — ✓ (Most Important)

   b. Basic science researchers? — ✓ (Least Important)

6. Is it important for you to have a particular grading system?

   a. Letter grade — ✓ (Least Important)

   b. Honors/pass/no pass — ✓ (Most Important)

   c. Pass/no pass — ✓ (Most Important)

7. Are the breadth and type of pre-clinical electives important?

8. Is the sequence of course work a concern? — ✓ (Not Sure)

(continued)

	Most Important	Least Important	Not Sure
9. How important is early clinical exposure?	___	___	✓
10. How important are educational innovations such as			✓
a. Self-instruction?	___	___	___
b. Computer-assisted instruction?	___	✓	___
c. Case-based learning?	___	___	✓
d. Non-animal teaching methods?	___	✓	___

Clinical Education

	Most Important	Least Important	Not Sure
11. How important is the type of health care facilities and setting?	___	___	✓
12. How important is it that you have access to a certain patient population?	___	___	✓
13. How important is it that the school emphasize			
a. Primary care?	___	___	✓
b. Tertiary care?	___	___	✓
14. Is it important that you have the opportunity to do rotations at other institutions or abroad?	___	___	✓

Research and Other
Educational Opportunities

	Most Important	Least Important	Not Sure
15. How important are opportunities for involvement in research?	(___	___	✓
16. How important is it that you have access to and can take courses at other institutions (e.g., universities, schools of public health or social work, law schools, or research centers)?	___	___	✓
17. How important is the option of an additional professional degree (e.g., Ph.D., J.D., M.P.H.)?	___	✓	___

(continued)

	Most Important	Least Important	Not Sure
Student Composition and Social Life			
18. How important is the composition of the student body (e.g., ethnic diversity, specialty, or personal interests)?	✓	___	___
19. How important is the quality of student social life (student clubs and activities)?	___	✓	___
20. How important is it that students be involved in shaping the school's policies (e.g., through working on educational curriculum, admissions selection, or student government)?	___	___	✓
Location			
21. How important is the environment in which the school is located?	✓	___	___
22. How important is living in			
a. A large city?	✓	___	___
b. A small town?	___	___	___
c. A rural setting?	___	___	___
23. How important is it that you			
a. Live near campus?	✓	___	___
b. Get on-campus housing?	___	___	___
24. How important is the availability of			
a. Public transportation?	___	✓	___
b. Parking?	✓	___	___
Student Services and Resources			
25. How important are the following academic services?			
a. Academic assistance and tutoring	✓	✓	___
b. Note-taking services	✓	___	___

(continued)

	Most Important	Least Important	Not Sure
c. Assistance preparing for the National Medical Board Exam (NMBE)	✓	____	____
26. How important are the following student support services?			
a. Student ombudsperson	____	____	____
b. Student affairs office	____	____	____
c. Faculty advisor/mentor program	✓	____	____
d. Support network and services for women and ethnic minorities	✓	____	____
e. Personal (psychological and career counseling)	____	____	____
f. Peer counseling	____	____	✓
g. Self-help and support groups	✓	____	____
h. Legal services	____	____	____
27. How important are			
a. Library facilities?	✓	____	____
b. Day care facilities?	____	✓	____
c. Fitness facilities?	____	____	✓
Cost			
28. How important is			
a. The cost of the school?	____	____	✓
b. The amount and type of financial aid?	✓	____	____
29. How important is it that your spouse or family have certain benefits?	____	____	____
Faculty			
30. How important is it that students have close interaction with faculty?	✓	____	____
31. Is the composition of the faculty important to you (e.g., percent women or minority faculty)?	____	____	____

(continued)

What to Do with Your Responses

1. List all the factors that you considered important. Make note of the absolutes (the things that you can't do without). Add other qualities you are looking for in a medical school.

2. Jot down the questions that you were unsure of or need more information on. Make it a point to investigate these issues further.

3. Hold on to these lists. You will use them to narrow down your choices of schools. They also will provide questions you can ask in the interview.

---

you should not choose a medical school based solely on these rankings. Furthermore, even the best schools have a few weak academic departments. If you want to be an orthopedic surgeon, it doesn't help to attend a school with a notoriously weak orthopedics program, even if that school is one of the "best" in the country.

On the other hand, the academic reputation of a school in the medical community is important when you compete for a residency. If you plan to apply to competitive residency programs, then your medical school's reputation may help. In addition to reputation, look at other indices of academic quality, such as attrition rates, percentage of students getting one of their top three residency choices, or performance on the National Medical Board Exam, Parts 1 and 2.

Pre-Clinical Education

The pre-clinical years are the first two years of medical school, when you gain the principles of medical knowledge, primarily basic science.

EDUCATIONAL APPROACH

During the pre-clinical years, three approaches to medical education exist: the traditional basic sciences approach, the modern organ systems approach, and the case-based learning approach.

The majority of schools use the traditional approach to medical education. This method relies on lectures to teach the various basic science disciplines such as anatomy, physiology, or biochemistry. Faculty members from each department, most of whom are basic science researchers, teach the courses. The topics are broad, and the information is exhaustive. Consequently, students may spend up to eight hours a day during the week in class.

The advantage of this method is that most of this information is synthesized for you. Lectures combine slides with audio and sometimes video to reinforce the learning process. Most students study from their lecture notes rather than delve into detailed medical texts.

The downside of the traditional method is that you spend more time in a dark lecture hall. There is also a discontinuity of information. You learn about one subject without knowing how it fits into the whole picture of medical education: the breakdown of sugar by the body (biochemistry) means little to a student until she or he knows that it occurs in the liver (anatomy), how it affects the rest of the body (physiology), and what can happen when something is wrong (pathology).

To help students assimilate information in a broader context, some schools organize the pre-clinical curriculum according to organ systems (for example, the brain, blood, or gastrointestinal system). This allows you to think about one system (for example, blood) while covering many different subject areas (biochemistry, molecular biology, physiology, pathology of blood components). The organ systems approach still uses lectures to present the information.

Finally, there is the more innovative case-based learning approach to pre-clinical education. Schools that use this method have typically abandoned the traditional medical lecture. Instead, students meet for a few hours per week in small interactive learning groups. Principles of basic science and clinical medicine are learned by examining patient cases. It is up to the student to research independently the biochemistry, physiology, anatomy, and pathology of the case in question and to present this information to the small group. This shifts the educational responsibility from the lecturer to the students.

Students who have a strong will to learn and are highly disciplined may benefit from the case-based method. Many students believe that the student-faculty interaction with this method is also more cooperative and personal. Students are taught almost entirely by clinicians rather than by basic science researchers. As a result, they get immediate exposure to the clinical foundation of medicine.

Some students don't function well in a case-based setting. It requires that they read medical books that present information in tremendous detail. Students must be self-starters. Also, the National Medical Board Exam, Part 1 (a test that residency programs use to judge medical students' knowledge) is designed for students in traditional basic science schools. Students from case-based programs may have more difficulties with this exam.

Not all schools fall strictly within these three categories. Many traditional schools are revising their curriculum in the first two years to include some problem-based learning and clinical experience. For example, a biochemistry course may have one lecture on lipid transport and another that reviews a patient case related to this material, such as a case of hypercholesterolemia.

Another recent trend in medical education is incorporating small groups into a traditional curriculum, to discuss patient cases or medical research, to review the subject matter from a lecture, or to practice clinical skills.

PRE-CLINICAL ELECTIVES

Electives allow you to tailor your education according to your interests and provide a break from the routine of other classes. Topics are diverse, ranging from herbal medicine to the biochemistry of neurophysiology.

PRE-CLINICAL GRADING POLICY

Medical schools have several different approaches to grading students in the pre-clinical years: pass/no pass, honors/pass/no pass, letter grades, or evaluation-based grading. To encourage a cooperative learning environment and reduce stress, many schools are changing to a pass/no pass grading system (also referred to by students as P = M.D.). The idea is that if you do not have to compete for an A grade, you will collaborate with your classmates. You also will not be tempted to spit in your classmate's petri dish during microbiology lab.

The majority of schools use a slightly more hierarchical approach: the honors/pass/no pass system. This system allows residency programs to distinguish among students at a particular medical school. Unfortunately, it also reintroduces the element of competition into academics. Most students, however, feel okay about this system, since it's usually so difficult to get an honors grade that students stop trying after the first semester.

Then comes the traditional A–F grading system. A variant of this, the honors/high pass/pass/no pass, is found in schools that want to appeal to prospective medical school applicants while retaining their conservative philosophy.

Evaluation-based grading abandons performance categories altogether. In each course, students receive a written evaluation with specific feedback on areas needing improvement. This can provide a clearer picture of a student's strengths and weaknesses for both the student and prospective residency programs.

The grading system, in part, determines the learning environment. You should consider the type of environment in which you learn best when choosing a medical school.

OTHER DIFFERENCES IN THE PRE-CLINICAL YEARS

For some students, close interaction with faculty and the feeling that they are not just "another number" are important. Some students prefer a research emphasis; others are concerned with early clinical exposure. Some may want to know about opportunities for independent study or the sequence of course work. One student, for example, chose his medical school based on its sequencing of anatomy in the first year.

Clinical Education

The second half of medical school is the clinical years, when you gain the hands-on knowledge and skill that you need to be a physician. During the clinical years, you will spend most of your time on the wards, rotating from one medical specialty to another. Each rotation, or clerkship, lasts from two to ten weeks. During this time, you serve as a member of the medical team and work directly with patients, diagnosing and treating medical conditions under supervision.

The organization of the clinical years is similar in most schools. The most important differences among schools are the approaches to educating students, the core clerkship requirements and clinical facilities, and the number of electives available.

EDUCATIONAL APPROACH

The quality of your clinical education will depend in large part on the medical team with whom you work. Often, clinical education is built on the "old boy" philosophy that learning is best taught through intimidation. It involves a near-universal phenomenon known as pimping, where students are quizzed in front of peers and other doctors. Presumably, this encourages students to study consistently so they are not humiliated during the pimp session, while allowing the graders to assess medical knowledge. Some schools are now discouraging such practices for a more supportive environment in which students are allowed to volunteer information during rounds (when the students and doctors go over patients' problems).

CLINICAL REQUIREMENTS AND FACILITIES

Schools differ in the number of required "core" clerkships. At most schools, these include medicine, surgery, psychiatry, obstetrics and gynecology, pediatrics, and neurology. Most of these rotations are based in a hospital setting. The type and diversity of hospital facilities vary according to school, including university-owned hospitals, public and private hospitals, Veterans Administration hospitals, or health maintenance organizations.

Increasingly, medical schools are moving away from hospital-based clerkships with their emphasis on acute care or end-stage disease. Many medical schools now require a clerkship in primary care or ambulatory medicine based in a clinic or office setting. The advantages of ambulatory care requirements are that they give students a perspective on the whole range of patient problems; allow students to see various stages of disease development; and emphasize continuity of care and preventive health. The disadvantage is that they take away from potential elective time for students.

CLINICAL ELECTIVES

Clinical electives are blocks of time when the student can work in different departments within the medical school, at other institutions, or with international programs. They allow students to look at prospective hospitals and residency programs and provide the opportunity to explore different cultures and patient populations both domestically and abroad. Schools vary in the number of "away" rotations they allow (anywhere from four weeks to a year). If this possibility interests you, investigate the flexibility of the clinical curriculum at the school you plan to attend.

CLINICAL GRADING POLICY

During the third and fourth years on the wards, nearly all schools use a tiered grading system to evaluate you—usually a combination of honors/pass/no pass with written evaluations. At the end of four years, the Dean of Student Affairs at your school reviews your evaluations from the wards and incorporates the information into a more concise "Dean's Letter."

Performance in the clinical years is probably the most important factor for residency program admission. This is particularly true for schools that use a pass/no pass policy in the first two years.

Research

Many schools offer research opportunities for students during the summer or on a part-time basis during the year. A few schools even require a research project before graduation. Students who are considering a research career in medicine may wish to apply to the Medical Scientist programs that are available at many universities. These programs offer students the opportunity to attend medical school while doing research for their Ph.D. degree.

Joint Degree Programs

Some students pursue additional degrees while in medical school—the Ph.D., M.S., M.A., J.D., or M.P.H. You may do this either through a joint degree program at the medical school or on your own. The ease and the practicality of the latter will depend on the flexibility of the school's curriculum and the proximity to other universities.

Consider the time commitment when planning a second degree. People with an interest in pursuing the medicolegal field (getting a law degree) or medical research (getting a Ph.D. degree) may be looking at an investment of up to nine years, simply to graduate. Obviously, then, you should speak with a counselor and also with other students before you commit yourself to this path. Completing a Masters in Public Health (M.P.H.) degree is a less burdensome time commitment. In fact, many programs will allow you to complete the M.D. and the M.P.H. degrees within the same amount of time normally required to graduate from medical school.

Working toward an additional degree can affect your financial aid package. This is good news for aspiring M.D./Ph.D. students—some programs are fully financed, including living stipends. However, if you pursue a joint M.D./M.S. or M.D./M.P.H. program, you will usually be paying for it yourself, typically in the form of increased loans.

Student Composition and Social Life

At any medical school with a reasonable class size, you can expect to find a diverse student population. Still, each school has its own character and will attract certain types of students. A primary care–oriented school, for example, is more likely to attract students interested in international and public health issues.

There is often a correlation between the character of the faculty and the students. The reason is obvious. A conservative school with a traditional academic curriculum will attract conservative faculty members who will select and mold like-minded students. If you studied art as an undergraduate and are interested in community empowerment and socialized health systems, this may not be a place you want to call home for the next four years.

Women and students who are of an ethnic or racial minority will want to consider carefully the composition of the student body and faculty. Not only will this determine your support network, it will profoundly affect your learning environment.

Student involvement in campus life is another consideration. Many schools have a number of committees that include student representation—ethics committees, faculty liaison groups, the educational curriculum committee, the admissions committee, and others. Where students have an effect on university policy and are involved with issues and with one another, there tends to be higher student morale. You also can determine how lively (or lame) the student body is by looking at the type and extent of clubs on campus.

Location

SIZE OF THE AREA

If you are a person who thrives on social activity, you may be most happy in an urban environment like New York or Chicago. Some people feel out of joint in cities and would be better off in a small town. For students who are parents, it may be important to live in a quiet and crime-free environment.

For some students, the size of the area in which their school is located can limit the type of medicine they can pursue. A disadvantage of studying in a small town during the clinical years is the low number of patients per student. Students who want a larger patient load and exposure to a variety of health problems should investigate schools in the city. A student with an interest in a specialized field, such as neurosurgery, would probably have to limit the choice of schools to an urban setting. To secure a residency in a competitive specialty such as neurosurgery, a student needs prior clinical experience in the field, including exposure to rare and complicated cases. The schools with the best tertiary care facilities (a hospital with highly trained experts and specialized equipment) are usually in larger cities.

On the other hand, a small town may be perfect for someone who is interested in rural health care. Many small town schools also offer clinical training in a nearby urban setting to give students exposure to a range of health problems and a greater patient volume.

POPULATION CHARACTERISTICS
Every geographic area in the United States, whether a small town or large city, has its own unique personality, defined in part by the socio-economic, cultural, and ethnic characteristics of its people. When examining a school, you should ask yourself if you are committed to working with the people in these areas, whether they be rural migrant workers, homosexuals, veterans, or elderly people.

LOCAL ENVIRONMENT
The environment of a school includes everything from the spirit of the people to the colors of the city. It is what makes a school unique: the energy level of the faculty, the expressions on students' faces, the way the sun reflects on the trees when you look out the library window.

What do you value in an environment? Perhaps you like museums, beautiful architecture, or parks. Maybe you prefer to be close to the ocean or within a quick drive of the mountains. Don't overlook these factors when choosing a medical school. Remember, you'll spend a significant number of your waking hours for the next four years within a few blocks of the campus. It ought to be a place where you feel at home.

Student Resources and Services

Schools vary in the type and quality of student resources and services. Almost all schools offer basic resources such as the Office of Curricular Affairs (the coordinating center for student events and activities); Dean of Student Affairs (an academic administrator, advisor, and evaluator of students); the Financial Aid Office and an Office of Minority Affairs (the center for recruitment and support of minority students).

Some schools also have an ombudsperson (a person who serves as a student advocate and mediator in academic disputes or student problems) and faculty mentors (faculty members who provide guidance and support throughout the four years). Most schools also provide psychological services (personal counseling, support groups, stress management seminars), health services (acute care, birth control, immunizations), legal services (tenant-landlord disputes, wills), academic services (tutoring, note-taking services and assistance preparing for the National Board Exam), and services for students with disabilities (mobility assistance, reading and note-taking assistance, special test-taking services).

The type and quality of student services and resources will vary from one school to the next, so each student should investigate this beforehand. Other resources that students should investigate include library and computer facilities, day care centers, and recreational centers.

The Cost

The cost of medical school, while expensive, should not deter you if you truly want to become a physician. All students who need financial aid will receive it; how much and what kind will vary according to the school and the extent of financial need.

Your expenses in medical school include

* Tuition
* Student fees (use of the student union, health center, gym, and the like)
* Student expenses (books, equipment, and related educational expenses)

- Living expenses (housing, utilities, food, clothing, car, and social expenses)

For state residents at state schools, the cost of tuition is a less important factor. The state subsidizes students' medical education and provides additional grants for state residents with extreme financial limitations. This is not so with private and out-of-state schools. In fact, tuition at private schools can be sixty to seventy thousand dollars more than the tuition of state schools over four years.

Living expenses also add to the cost of medical school. The annual cost of living can vary from seven to twenty thousand dollars per year depending on the location of the school and your lifestyle. Some schools provide special housing for married students and help cover other expenses such as day care or medical insurance. The student with a family should consider these benefits when evaluating the entire financial aid package.

The type of financial aid varies according to the school and your financial need. A financial aid package may include grants, low-interest loans, and high-interest loans. Most students will have a combination of all three.

To be eligible for federal grants and low-interest (government subsidized) loans, you must meet federal eligibility requirements. These vary from year to year. The 1994 federal requirements, broadened under President Clinton's education package, state that all graduate or professional students are regarded as independent and are eligible for federal aid under these conditions:

- Must have documented financial need
- Must be enrolled at least half-time and making satisfactory academic progress
- Must not be in default on a loan or owe a refund on an educational grant
- Must register with the Selective Service, if male

For medical school, scholarships are scarce. Most students rely on loans from a federal source, a private source, or both. Unfortunately, low-interest federal loans have a ceiling. The federal Stafford Student Loan has a borrowing limit of $8,500 per year with about an 8.25 percent interest rate. The federal Perkins Loan has a cap of $5,000 per year with a 5 percent interest rate.

Other federal loan sources are available for students willing to commit to a primary care field of medicine (such as general internal medicine, pediatrics, general family practice, and soon, obstetrics and gynecology). There are penalties for failing to follow through with your commitments, so this is not a good source of income if you are unsure. Minority and low-income student loans may be available from your state as well as some private institutions.

Loans from private sources are extremely easy to get and usually have high ceilings but, depending on the federal interest rate, can have a higher annual percentage rate than private bank loans. Most students with these loans will double their medical education costs before paying them off because of this high interest rate. This is the real reason that public schools are so much more attractive for the prudent medical school shopper. After all, if you can meet most of your tuition and living expense with a low-interest loan, you will be making payments mostly on your medical school expenses and not on interest.

As Facika noted,

Cost was a factor for me. After all, you need to know how much debt you can assume and how you might be locked in for the next twenty years because of that debt.

SEEKING MORE INFORMATION

By now you should have a preliminary understanding of the characteristics that distinguish medical schools. You also have an idea of what you want in a medical school. If we have been successful, a dozen other questions will be buzzing in your head. Obviously, we can't answer all these questions in this chapter. What we can do is steer you in the right direction, to the people and places where you will find answers to your questions.

The search for "objective" information about medical school is much like the quest for the Holy Grail. Sift carefully through the information you hear. Whenever possible, get information from the source rather than from the pre-medical circuit.

Find up-to-date books and articles on the subject of medical education and admission to medical school. An excellent source of information is the *Medical School Admissions Requirements* (published annually by the Association of American Medical Colleges). This contains basic information on each of the 126 AAMC-accredited schools, including a short summary of their curriculum and academic philosophy, course and other requirements, selection factors, degree programs offered, tuition and fees, and types of financial aid available. Also included are recent statistics about the applicant pool, as well as application deadlines, costs, and other information on admissions. This book is factual and dry, so don't expect to discover anything about the character of the school or its students by reading it. However, it is extremely useful as a reference while applying and may help you begin to narrow down the list of schools that interest you most.

Consider a membership in the National Pre-Health Student Association (NPSA), P.O. Box 1518, Champaign, Illinois 61824-1518. Its quarterly newsletter provides current tidbits on what is happening at various medical schools.

Most undergraduate institutions have a career center with additional resources that are useful to pre-medical students. At many schools, they have medical school catalogs. Often there are questionnaires from former students now attending medical school that provide individual perspectives on the transition to medical school.

WHERE ELSE CAN YOU GO FOR HELP?

Pre-medical Advisor

The most obvious source of information about medical schools is a pre-medical advisor. If you are lucky, you will have an advisor who is in contact with various schools, has up-to-date information, and can offer advice as well as inform you about events that are of interest to pre-medical students.

You don't need a specific agenda to request a meeting with the pre-medical advisor. If you are already into the process of seriously considering medical schools, you might ask about schools in the area and the competitiveness of their admission processes. Ask how students in the past went about deciding upon a medical school, where they enrolled, and whether they were happy with their choices. See if the advisor can refer you to other people at the medical school or elsewhere who would be available to talk with you.

You should maintain a friendly working relationship with your pre-medical advisor, for you will need his or her help and a letter of recommendation when you are applying to medical schools. Remember though, your advisor is not the only resource available to you. Nor are advisors the final word on matters of pre-medical or medical education. You may wind up with an uninterested faculty member whose only resource is an AAMC manual and a few old medical school catalogs. If you find your pre-medical advisor's office to be a dead end, you can pursue other channels.

Medical Students

During your undergraduate years you should try to discuss your interests and concerns about medical school with many different medical students. They are usually more comprehensive than a medical school catalog and more candid than a pre-medical advisor, and probably have more insight into the mechanics of a medical education than all others combined.

Medical students are a group of diverse people with a variety of lifestyles, interests, and opinions. Each person will have unique insights about medical school and the decisions they have made. Ask what they would do differently if they had to choose a medical school again.

There are many ways you can gain exposure to the medical school environment and meet medical students and faculty with whom to interact. If you are attending a university with an affiliated medical school, you have access to a wide range of activities on the medical school campus and may even enroll in some elective courses there. There are pre-medical clubs that sponsor trips to area medical schools. These trips allow you to meet medical students in an informal environment, follow a medical student for a day, or even spend the night at his or her house.

Admissions or Student Affairs Office

Call the Admissions or Student Affairs Office at schools you are interested in. Ask if they have tour days for interested pre-medical students or if you could meet with a student and attend classes with that person.

Make an effort to meet students with common interests. Medical school catalogs will list student organizations that have formed around special interests. For example, if you are interested in health care in Mexican-American communities, look up organizations such as Chicanos for Health Education (CHE) and find medical students who are involved in this organization.

No matter what type of person you are and what background you come from, you can find a medical school that resonates with your character, lifestyle, and goals.

11

THE APPLICATION PROCESS

It is human nature to speculate and create stories about those aspects of life that are shrouded in mystery—the dawn of civilization, the movements of the heavens, the nature of matter. To pre-medical students, the process of being accepted to medical school is among life's great mysteries.

Most students know little about the necessary steps for applying to medical school and even less about how these applications are processed on the other side. At the same time, everyone has an opinion. If you travel in pre-medical circles long enough, you'll hear it all: what admissions committees *really* want to hear in the personal statement, how to dress for your interview, what experiences will get you the "fat envelope" (the letter of acceptance).

Applicants can be misled by such speculation. One pre-medical student was told by another applicant not to appear too compassionate on the personal statement. His reasoning? Doctors should give a distant, impartial impression. Another student purposely deleted her current employment on the application (she was working three jobs). She didn't want the admissions committee to think that she was financially strapped.

When going through the application process, try to avoid thinking too much about "what the admissions committee wants." Medical school admissions committees do *not* look for a stereotyped applicant with a standard combination of courses, extracurricular activities, or grades. They value *individuals*. Furthermore, since each school has a distinct mission, the admissions committee at each school will value different types of individuals.

The goal of the application process is to convey your individuality, to infuse your life and experiences into the pages of the application. Rather than create an image of the ideal applicant (who may or may not exist), use the application to present an honest and clear depiction of *yourself*.

UNDERSTANDING THE ADMISSIONS PROCESS

Enough with the guesswork. What's the admissions process really about? If you are serious about applying and getting into medical school, you owe it to yourself to get the facts.

There are several phases to the admissions process: the primary application, secondary applications, the interview, and then (hopefully) acceptance. It tends to be a long and involved process. It can also be incredibly frustrating if you don't know what's happening as you're going through it.

In the following sections, we explain the various procedures involved in applying to medical school so that you know what is expected of you and can plan for the months ahead. We also try to shed some light on the admissions process itself. If you don't find a particular answer here, we encourage you to seek other sources.

Stage One: The Primary Application

Most medical schools in the United States use a centralized application service for the primary medical school application—either the American Medical Colleges Application Service (AMCAS) for allopathic medical schools or the American Association of Colleges of Osteopathic Medicine Application Service (AACOMAS) for osteopathic medical schools. These application centers serve as intermediaries between the applicant and participating medical schools.

Applicants can apply to participating schools by completing the AMCAS or AACOMAS primary application. This application requests basic information such as the schools you've attended, your GPA, extracurricular activities and employment, summer experiences, honors and awards, and a personal statement. Applicants forward official transcripts and a fee (depending on the number of schools to which you apply) to the application center.

The application center processes the primary application materials by checking that the information is complete and correct and forwards a computerized application summary to each of the schools indicated. This system relieves the school of much of the paperwork and the logistical burden of processing applications. It also makes it easier for the applicant, since you can apply to many schools by filing a single primary application.

Some allopathic medical schools do not participate in AMCAS. If you are interested in applying to these schools, you will need to fill out a separate primary application. Information about the type of primary application for each medical school and where to obtain non-AMCAS applications can be found in a recent copy of *Medical School Admission Requirements* (MSAR).

THE TIME FRAME

AMCAS accepts applications from June 15 until November 15 of the year preceding matriculation. AACOMAS accepts applications beginning June 1 throughout the admissions cycle. However, if you wait until after December to apply, you might miss a deadline for a particular school or find that the class is already filled.

Both application services notify you when they receive your application materials and begin processing. If your application is complete, it will take about four to six weeks to process and forward your application to individual schools. If anything is missing from the application—if you forget to sign the last page, or if your transcripts don't arrive—it will mean a delay. The application center will send you a computer profile of your application and a list of the schools to which it was sent. Individual schools will notify you when they receive your application from the AMCAS or AACOMAS center.

Non-AMCAS schools have their own schedules for accepting and processing applications. The MSAR book and the AACOM information book listed in the Reference section have the important dates for each school.

EARLY DECISIONS

Many allopathic medical schools participate in Early Decision Programs (EDP). Applicants who have a preference for one school and are strong candidates may wish to apply for early decision. To qualify as an EDP candidate, you must submit your AMCAS application before August 1 *and select only one school.* EDP applicants are notified by October 1 if they are accepted to this school.

If you apply to a school for early decision and are accepted, you must accept the offer of admission. AMCAS applicants who are not accepted through the EDP may apply to other schools after October 15.

The deadlines for EDP applicants at osteopathic schools vary. Check with each school and apply to AACOMAS at least six weeks before the early decision date(s). This may be as early as June 15 in the application cycle.

THE INITIAL SCREENING

In the initial screening, schools may use either a formula or non-formula-based method to evaluate applicants. A formula-based method is empirical. Various factors may be plugged into an equation—MCAT scores and GPA, difficulty of your undergraduate course work, selectivity of your undergraduate institution, and state residence, among others. Applicants are then ranked or assigned to categories such as "Immediate Interview," "Further Processing," "Hold," or "Reject." In a non-formula-based method, similar factors are considered by nonempirical means.

Because of the sheer volume of applications, most schools will only evaluate certain aspects of your application in the initial screening. For the majority of schools, the early emphasis is on academic ability, with particular attention to undergraduate GPA and MCAT scores. Schools may evaluate these credentials in various ways: weighing science and nonscience GPA separately; examining grades in particular courses; or considering improvement over time. Some schools will consider other markers of academic achievement in the initial screening, such as research, special projects, and honors and awards.

Less commonly, a school will evaluate an application in its entirety in the initial screening. For example, along with the academic information (GPA, MCAT scores), a committee may read personal statements. This is not practical at most schools because it requires an enormous investment of resources to process this information on every applicant.

We often hear applicants say that MCAT scores and GPA are the only things that matter when it comes to the medical school admissions process. In some circumstances, this may be true. For example, an applicant with very poor grades, even if this person has done more service than Mother Teresa, will be eliminated in the initial screening at most schools.

The opposite, however, is not true: high MCAT scores and GPA do not guarantee admission. A very high academic achiever who focuses on her studies to the exclusion of all else is not an ideal applicant.

Proving your academic competence is a hurdle that you must pass early in the admissions process. After that, other factors may be more important. As one medical student (who also sat on an admissions committee) explained, "At some point, applicants need to show who they are, and that comes from their life experiences."

Those aspects of your application that provide greater insight into who you are—the personal statement, letters of recommendation, and the interview—are examined more closely in the later stages of the application process.

ROLE OF ETHNICITY, SOCIOECONOMIC CLASS, OR GENDER

Race/ethnicity, socioeconomic status, and gender are also a part of the larger spectrum of who you are. They provide insight into your life experiences, particular challenges, and assets that you may bring to the medical community.

These factors are considered, along with many others, usually after the initial screening. They help the committee to evaluate a person's level of achievement by taking into account the context of the person's life. Race/ethnicity, gender, or class may also be important to a school's mission, to ensure equal opportunity in medicine and to enhance medical education by cultivating diversity in the class and ultimately in the practicing community.

Stage Two: The Secondary Application

Individual schools request further information in a secondary application. This includes, at a minimum, letters of recommendation and, at many schools, an essay (plus an additional fee). Some schools use the secondary application to examine in more detail your course work, employment, or extracurricular experiences, or your suitability for that particular medical school and its mission. Some schools request a photo "for identification purposes."

WHO RECEIVES A SECONDARY APPLICATION?

This will vary from school to school. Some schools send secondary applications without screening the primary application. Anyone who completes the primary application is automatically mailed the secondary application.

Most schools, however, have an initial screening before they send secondary applications. A few very selective schools send secondaries only to the 10–20 percent of applicants they intend to interview. Other schools use a passive screening process. They invite all applicants to complete the secondary application, but they discourage the less promising applicants from continuing by using carefully phrased form letters.

In general, if you get a secondary, it's a good sign. If you want to know how good a sign it *really* is, call the admissions office to ask how many secondaries they send out.

THE TIME FRAME

If there is no screening process, you should receive a secondary application shortly after the school receives your primary application. Otherwise, the initial screening may take weeks or months after your primary application is received (including MCAT scores). Mid-fall is the busiest time for admissions offices, so expect a longer wait at that time. Sometimes it depends on your qualifications: high-priority applicants may receive secondaries more quickly than others.

If you are notified that your primary application was received and you do not hear from the school within six to eight weeks, call the admissions offices of the schools you listed on your application to make sure that something has not gone awry (usually it just means that the school is slow).

Stage Three: The Interview

The average allopathic medical school grants around 600 interviews per application cycle—less than one-third of the applicant pool. Some larger allopathic medical schools may conduct as many as 1,800 interviews (see Chapter 12).

Osteopathic schools tend to grant fewer interviews per applicant pool. For example, one osteopathic school interviews approximately 200 applicants out of an applicant pool of 4,000. They accept 150 of these interviewees for a class size of 100.

THE TIME FRAME

Schools conduct interviews from late fall until March or April. On average, applicants are invited for an interview within four to six weeks after the secondary application materials are in. Again, this is highly variable. You may be surprised to find a message on your answering machine a week later from one school, while your application collects dust at another.

Stage Four: Acceptance, Wait List, or Rejection

ACCEPTANCE

Schools make as many offers of admission as are necessary to fill the class (often two to three times the size of the class). Most schools have a policy of rolling admissions, which means that they accept applicants throughout the admissions cycle.

According to AAMC guidelines, schools may begin sending offers of admission after October 15 (with the exception of EDP candidates, whom they must notify by October 1). By March 15, schools should make offers of admission equal to at least half their class size. Additional guidelines regarding acceptance procedures for the first-year class are detailed in the AMCAS or AACOMAS application booklet.

To accept an offer of admission, you must file a letter of intent, including a deposit, usually around $100. This allows you to hold a place in that class. Students are allowed to hold more than one acceptance while deciding between schools (or waiting to hear from another school). If you decide against a particular school, or accept a spot at another higher-priority school, you should *immediately* notify the school that you are dropping. That way you free up the spot for someone else, who may be anxiously awaiting a response.

After May 15, you can reserve a spot at only one allopathic medical school. Osteopathic medical schools have comparable policies.

WAIT LIST

Applicants who are qualified but perhaps not as competitive may be placed on a wait list. This allows a school to survey applicants over the entire application cycle in order to select the best candidates.

For the applicant, the wait list can be unnerving—an ambiguous category that throws a wrench into all other decisions. What happens if you are wait-listed at your first-choice school and the wait lasts into the summer months? Do you go ahead and pay registration fees at another school where you were accepted? Do you plan your housing in the event of last-minute acceptance?

It's difficult to interpret your odds of acceptance at any one school where you are wait-listed. Some schools move quickly through the wait list. Others have hundreds of applicants waiting and only go through twelve before they fill the class. It depends on the school, the year, and where you are on the list. Before you make any major decisions, consult with the people in the admissions office at the school where you are wait-listed. Remember to be nice when requesting information. While you won't get any definitive answers, they may provide some inkling as to where you stand. At the very least, they should explain the process to you. Continue to make plans but be flexible.

REJECTION

The number of people applying to medical school has risen steadily each year since 1989. Currently, twice as many people apply to medical school as there are available spots. What this means is that each year thousands of qualified applicants are turned away. Even if you are highly qualified, you most likely will not be accepted to all the schools to which you apply.

If you are not accepted at any of the schools to which you apply, you need to examine why: Was it simply a matter of poor planning in the application process, or are you lacking the fundamental credentials and experience to be a strong candidate?

It may simply be that you didn't apply to enough schools or the right type of school. On the other hand, there may be substantial reasons to doubt whether you are prepared for medical school or suited to be a doctor—deficits in your academic record or too little experience.

At the end of it all, you must ask yourself the same hard questions that an admissions committee asks: Are you making a mature and informed decision to become a doctor? Are you academically prepared to handle medical school? Does a career in medicine fit with your personality and your lifestyle?

REAPPLYING

If all the answers to the preceding questions are affirmative in your mind, you may decide to reapply later. As many as one-fourth of all accepted applicants in any year are applying for the second time. Consider, however, that the only way to be accepted to medical school the second time is if something changes—your qualifications and experience, your application strategies, or preferably both.

Before you reapply, contact the schools where you were rejected. You may do this by writing a letter to the Dean of Admissions inquiring about the reasons your application was rejected and ways that you could strengthen your candidacy. Some students decide to spend a year working in a medical setting or doing research while they reapply. You may need to retake the MCAT or take more courses. Some people benefit from enrolling in a postbaccalaureate pre-medical program (see Chapter 5).

You should concentrate on ways to improve your application strategy. For example, Lloyd, as an older applicant, received helpful advice from one of his interviewers about schools that accept a lot of "nontraditional" students. The second time around, he targeted those schools that were more likely to regard him favorably.

APPEALS

In a very few cases, it may be warranted to appeal the committee's decision and request a reevaluation. Making such an appeal should not be taken lightly. However, if you believe that there are extenuating circumstances that require special consideration by the admissions committee, you may wish to address these concerns in writing to the Dean of Admissions. You are at least guaranteed due process.

THE ADMISSIONS COMMITTEE

Now you know about the process, but what about the people behind it?

The medical school admissions committee is often talked about as if it were a single entity. In reality, the committee is an eclectic group of people with different backgrounds and interests, from different sectors of the university and the community at large. Schools of medicine strive to achieve diversity of ethnicity and gender, and representation of different areas of medicine on the committee. These people provide unique perspectives on applicants and reflect the multifaceted interests of the school.

Members of the admissions committee are selected either by the Dean of Admissions or by a standing committee. Members usually serve for at least three years and fulfill various roles on the committee.

Most members are part of the full-time faculty at the school of medicine, from the basic sciences and clinical departments. Medical students may also be included on the admissions committee. Some schools invite practicing physicians from the community, and other health professionals such as nurses and health educators, to serve on the committee.

Occasionally, medical school admissions committees may include people from outside the medical circuit, such as a professor of philosophy or individuals from the community.

Some schools have psychiatrists who are members of the faculty and serve as behavioral experts or consultants when there are concerns about the psychiatric history of the applicant.

The Dean of Admissions is the key person who elaborates and carries out a school's admissions policies and procedures. This person takes the lead in developing strategies that support the school's individual mission and that meet national and state guidelines. The Dean oversees the activities of the committee and ensures that the admissions process runs smoothly. He or she must approve the recommendations of the committee to admit an applicant.

Admissions committees may be structured in a number of ways. The committee may function as a single entity evaluating each applicant, or the committee may be broken into subcommittees.

Commonly today, a medical school committee consists of working groups (subcommittees). Reviewers in each working group have special experience and insight specific to the applicants they will be evaluating. Eventually, the recommendations of the working group are passed to other groups for evaluation.

MINORITIES IN MEDICINE—
INCREASING OPPORTUNITIES

Since the 1960s, there have been strong efforts to rectify racial, social, and class inequities in our society and our educational system. Affirmative action policies grew out of this movement and have, to some extent, been successful in creating diversity on our campuses of higher learning. Still, certain groups are significantly underrepresented in medical school enrollment: African Americans, Mainland Puerto Ricans, Mexican Americans, and Native Americans.

The shortage of minority health professionals is of particular concern to the medical community. It is one factor that contributes to deteriorating health care services in minority and economically disadvantaged communities. There is a need for physicians, teachers, and researchers from every background who are willing to serve—and who will be sensitive to—the health needs of an ethnically diverse population.

Project 3000 by 2000, developed by the AAMC in the late 1980s, encourages medical schools to expand educational opportunities for underrepresented and low-income students. The goal is to increase the number of entering minority medical students in the nation to 3000 by the year 2000.

The environment at most medical schools has undergone a transformation in the last few decades. How far we have come can best be illustrated by this story, told by one medical student:

> One day after dissection, our anatomy professor pulled a bunch of us over. He had this picture taken in the same anatomy lab in the 1960s. They were just like us, hundreds of eager, bright first-year medical students kneeling over cadavers—only they were all white men in suits. Here we were—two black guys, one white woman, and our professor, who is gay. I thought, "Dang, things have changed."

Things have changed. Unfortunately, the gains are uneven. While some schools have successfully ushered the ethnic diversity of society into the academic community, others cling to the status quo. Political pressure to disband affirmative action may alter this landscape even further in the future.

Minority and low-income students should carefully investigate their options when deciding where to apply and attend medical school. Recruitment programs and support services for low-income and minority applicants vary from one school to the next. Some schools boast an oasis of services, a gracious community, and strong support networks, whereas at others, once you get there, you're on your own. For more information, consult the MSAR book.

If you are a minority applicant, make yourself known to the Office of Minority Affairs at each school as early as possible. That way, when you apply, you are more than just a name in a stack of papers.

The Medical Minority Applicant Registry (Med-Mar) program provides a direct conduit for underrepresented and low-income applicants to make contact with medical schools. Through the Med-Mar program, applicants may circulate their biographical information to the minority affairs offices of participating U.S. medical schools and other organizations that request it.

Minority and low-income applicants may use this service free of charge. You begin by filling out a questionnaire at the time of the MCAT. Participating schools will contact you to request more information. To find out more about the Med-Mar program, write to Minority Student Information Clearing House, Association of American Medical Colleges, 2450 N Street, N.W., Washington, D.C. 20037-1126.

THE COST OF APPLYING

Money should be the last thing on your mind while applying to medical school. Yet the cost of applying—application fees, travel costs, lost work—can be a potential roadblock for many applicants.

AMCAS and AACOMAS will waive the application fee for people whose extreme financial limitations would otherwise prevent them from applying to medical school. Fee waiver request forms are included in the application packet. To apply, you must send in financial statements from your parents and certification from a financial aid officer at your school. For AACOMAS waivers, contact COMP (Colleges of Osteopathic Medicine), 6110 Executive Blvd., Suite 405, Rockville, MD 20852.

Applicants should submit requests for a fee waiver early. It may be four to eight weeks before a request is approved, and until then your application will not be processed.

If you get a fee waiver from AMCAS or AACOMAS, most schools will also waive additional fees associated with the secondary application. Otherwise, you may appeal directly to the school in a letter, with your financial materials, that explains your difficulty in paying the secondary fee.

By far, the biggest financial dent will be for interviews. For most schools, you will need to travel to the school (a few offer regional interviews). Costs of travel and housing can be reduced by scheduling interviews at schools in the same geographic area at the same time. Some schools also offer housing for applicants (see Chapter 12).

WHERE TO APPLY

To be realistic, not everyone can apply to the most selective schools and expect to get in. Many schools will not consider applicants below a certain cutoff point for MCAT scores and GPA. To save time and hefty application fees, you should make strategic and informed choices about where to apply (see Chapter 10).

Even with a well-thought-out application strategy, there is still an element of luck in the admissions process. Because of this, and the intense competition, the average student applies to ten schools. Some applicants go to an extreme—they apply to a gazillion schools in hopes of increasing their chances (it doesn't appreciably). The question of how many schools to apply to will depend on your qualifications and how carefully you select the schools. Here are our recommendations for applying:

- Apply to schools that represent a range of competitiveness. Even if you think your chances of acceptance at one school are high, do not count on anything. Include more than one "safety school."
- Apply to the schools in your state. State schools give priority to in-state students. Most private schools also receive some state subsidies in exchange for educating more state residents. If there is not a medical school in your state of residence, there may be reciprocal arrangements with neighboring states.

- Apply to the schools that are compatible with your personal interests, career goals, and lifestyle. This makes sense for your own happiness, but it will also help you get into medical school. A research school is naturally attracted to the budding undergraduate scientist, whereas a school in a culturally diverse urban area may appreciate students with specific language skills. Some schools have a special commitment to ethnic diversity or to nontraditional students.

By applying to schools that are appropriate for you in terms of your interests, experiences, and qualifications, you increase your chances of admission. This doesn't mean you should limit yourself only to those schools for which you fit the model student profile. Each school values some diversity. But recognize what you have that is unique, and go where the opportunities are greatest.

GETTING STARTED

In order to stay on top of everything, you'll need to develop a time line for your tasks.

In the following box, we have outlined important milestones in the application process. We've started twenty months before the time you wish to enter medical school. This will help you remember some of the things you need to do and keep track of your deadlines. We begin with a lot of structure to get you started, recognizing that by the middle of the admissions cycle everyone is at different points.

If you are not an undergraduate, are applying for an Early Decision Program, or are studying in a postbaccalaureate program, your schedule of activities may be different. We've included some space so that you can adapt the schedule to suit your individual needs.

COMMON SENSE WE LEARNED AT THE DEPARTMENT OF MOTOR VEHICLES (THAT CAN HELP YOU APPLY TO MEDICAL SCHOOL)

Have you ever tried to beat the Department of Motor Vehicles (DMV)? You ignore a few parking tickets or don't bother with the

A Typical Timetable for the Admissions Process

Approximately Twenty Months Before Beginning Medical School (January–February)

Important Dates and Deadlines

February 1—AMCAS and MCATs applications available.

- Read
    - ____ Chapter 9 (The MCAT), Chapter 10 (Choosing a Medical School), and Chapter 11 (The Application Process) of this book.
- Plan
    - ____ Decide where you want to apply to medical school. If undecided, visit or contact schools for more information.
    - ____ Meet with your pre-medical advisor to get information about the application process and to discuss plans and strategies.
- Activities
    - ____ Organize your application filing system.
    - ____ Obtain your AMCAS or AACOMAS application.
    - ____ Request applications from non-AMCAS schools.
    - ____ Begin studying for the MCAT; take a review course or practice exams, if necessary.
    - ____ Prepare a personal profile and other information to be sent to those who will write your letters of recommendation.
    - ____ Request your personal copy of undergraduate transcripts for all schools attended.
    - ____ Other _____

Approximately Eighteen to Sixteen Months Before Beginning Medical School (March–May)

Important Dates and Deadlines

March 15—AMCAS accepts official transcripts.

Before March 15—Last day to mail MCAT application for April test date.

- Read _____
- Plan
    - ____ Meet with pre-medical advisor to review plans.
    - ____ Investigate costs and financial aid at the schools you are interested in.

(continued)

____ Plan for how you will meet the costs of applying, visiting, and interviewing.
- Activities
  ____ Visit medical schools, if necessary, to finalize choices.
  ____ Register to take the MCAT (check exact deadline in MCAT announcement).
  ____ Apply for fee waivers, if applicable. Note deadlines for applying, which may be before application deadlines.
  ____ Make final MCAT preparations; take the exam.
  ____ Photocopy your applications(s) and begin entering information in draft form. Identify the information you will need to obtain to complete the application.
  ____ Begin writing your application essay(s). Be relaxed, let your ideas percolate. Put away the first draft; pull out and rewrite it one month later.
  ____ Obtain feedback on your essay and rewrite again.
  ____ Request your letters of recommendation from individuals or from your pre-medical committee.
  ____ Other _____

Approximately Fifteen to Thirteen Months Before Beginning Medical School (June–August)

Important Dates and Deadlines
June 1—AACOMAS accepts application materials.
June 15—AMCAS accepts application materials.
Early July—Schools begin to receive applications from AMCAS and AACOMAS.
August 1—All available AACOMAS fee waivers usually granted by this date.
August 15—AMCAS deadline for Early Decision Program (EDP).
- Read
  ____ Medical journals (for example, *New England Journal of Medicine*).
  ____ School catalogs, as you receive them.
  ____ _____
- Plan _____
- Activities
  ____ Complete applications and begin to submit according to deadlines. Meet the Early Decision Program deadline if you have chosen this route.

(continued)

____ Request that your schools send official transcripts to AMCAS or AACOMAS.

Approximately Twelve to Ten Months Before Beginning Medical School (September–October)

Important Dates and Deadlines

October 1—EDP acceptance notification by this date.

October 15—AMCAS applicants begin to receive notification of acceptance.

October 15–December 15—AMCAS application deadlines for individual medical schools.

- Read _____
- Plan

   ____ Plan course work for final year of undergraduate program, if applicable. Meet with pre-medical advisor, if necessary, to review these plans.

- Activities

   ____ Continue to research and obtain information about selected schools.

   ____ Contact references and thank them for their letters.

   ____ Prepare for essays on secondary applications.

   ____ Complete primary applications and submit (if you haven't already done so).

   ____ Complete secondary applications as they arrive.

   ____ Reassess goals based on preliminary feedback from medical schools.

   ____ Other _____

Approximately Nine to Seven Months Before Beginning Medical School (November–January)

Important Dates and Deadlines

December 1—Deadline for AMCAS fee waiver requests.

December 1–February 1—Regular AACOMAS application deadlines according to school.

- Read

   ____ Chapter 12 (The Interview) of this book.

- Plan

   ____ Begin preparing for interviews.

   ____ Continue to file secondary applications, if necessary.

(continued)

- Activities
  - ____ Last chance to file primary applications.
  - ____ Schedule interviews at appropriate times; arrange for transportation and housing for interviews.
  - ____ Write brief thank-you notes to interviewers at schools where you visited.
  - ____ Maintain contact with your pre-medical advisor regarding your secondaries and interviews.

Approximately Six to Five Months Before Beginning Medical School (February–March)

Important Dates and Deadlines
- Read _____
- Plan
  - ____ Finalize decision, if possible.
- Activities
  - ____ Revisit schools, if necessary, to make your final decision.
  - ____ Decline schools you have been accepted to that you do not wish to attend.
  - ____ Call or write people who wrote you letters of recommendation to inform them of your decision.

Approximately Four to Three Months Before Beginning Medical School (April–May)

Important Dates and Deadlines
- Activities
  - ____ Celebrate (or regroup, if necessary).
  - ____ Finalize financial arrangements.
  - ____ Make transportation and housing arrangements for school you will attend.
  - ____ If not accepted but on wait lists, make contingency plans for possible last-minute acceptance.

emissions check. We all know what happens. Extra fees, extra hassle, and wasted time.

Surviving the medical school application process is a bit like dealing with the DMV. You have to know where and when to expend your energy. Ahead of you are several challenges: (1) the challenge of being proactive; (2) the challenge of self-reflection; and (3) the challenge of bureaucracy and all its tedium. The more efficient you are in dealing with the bureaucracy, the more time and energy you have for the more productive work.

The following recommendations should help ease the application process and almost completely guarantee that you avoid common glitches like missed deadlines, delays, and dumb mistakes.

FOLLOW DIRECTIONS

Sound trivial? Each year thousands of applications are held up because applicants send in copies of forms (instead of the original as requested), or list schools in the wrong order, or leave a box unchecked. A school may get a beautifully written essay on the secondary application that has *nothing to do* with the question asked.

READ ALL THE MATERIALS

Before you go to the library or call the admissions office, read the material in front of you. Schools will often explain their application process and let you know when you will hear from them again. The school catalog is also a valuable source of information.

DOUBLE–CHECK EVERYTHING

Just because you request that your transcripts be sent, don't count on their reaching their destination. Anything that involves other people increases the chance that something could go wrong. Usually, you will receive a receipt from the schools when they receive materials (some schools are better than others about this). *Keep track of these receipts.* If you don't get notification, call the admissions office to check on your application.

MAKE COPIES OF EVERYTHING

Remember Murphy's law? There should be an addendum. Anything that can go wrong—if you do not make copies—will. Throughout the admissions process you will be preparing and sending out materials. Keep a copy of everything, particularly that computer disk with all your essays and personal statements on it.

DEVELOP A METHOD

This time it is the law of entropy. If you are not organized, you will soon be swimming in a sea of application forms of every color, 3 x 5 cards (to be self-addressed and stamped), and mail confirming and requesting different materials for half a dozen different applications.

Prevent chaos before it happens. Invest in a file crate. Keep a separate file folder for each application. Copy the timetable box in this chapter (or your adaptation of it) and post it in the front of your crate. Or buy an agenda book only for the application process. List goals and make a schedule. Keep notes of all telephone conversations, interviewers' names, directions to schools, and the like in this book. If you have your own system, stick to that, as long as you have a way to stay on top of work and deadlines before they pile up on you.

START EARLY
How many of you turn in papers just in the nick of time? You're stressed to the hilt, and afterward you're kicking yourself at the number of typos.

Do yourself a favor, be an early bird when it comes to the application process. Take another look at the timetable. You'll need time to complete your application, compose your essays, collect materials, schedule interviews and—most importantly—make decisions.

Need another reason? Murphy's law. Even the most meticulous applicants run into problems. Next to following our advice, the best assurance against complications is extra time.

COMPLETING THE AMCAS/AACOMAS APPLICATION

The first hurdle is the biggest—the primary application. To even call it an application downplays the effort required to complete this document. Consider the AMCAS application—the application itself is only four pages long, but the instruction booklet is sixty!

Your main task with the primary application is to condense information in a way that is both logical and pleasing to the eye. You also will need to obtain your academic transcripts and convert your grades to the AMCAS or AACOMAS grading scale—a logistical headache if you have been to different colleges.

Those with an eye for detail will fare well with the primary application. All the basic DMV rules apply: begin early, be methodical, and double-check your application.

If you wish, you can now file your AMCAS application using a diskette (AMCAS-E) provided by AMCAS that will operate on both the PC (Windows) and Macintosh computers. No hard (paper) copy will be required if you submit this diskette; you can thus avoid the frustration of typing everything perfectly into the boxes on the application form. This software will also permit applicants seeking a fee waiver to complete an AMCAS fee waiver request.

The Personal Statement

Students are often stumped about how to approach the application essay. The thought of writing a personal statement on one page is intimidating. The looming presence of the admissions committee makes it even more perplexing. How do you compose an essay about your life experiences, feelings, and motivations to become a doctor when your fate is tangled up with an unknown reader?

One student we know was recently struggling with this issue when applying to graduate school. She wanted to write a "smart" essay, but each attempt, an impressive but lifeless list of accomplishments, wound up in the wastebasket. So we asked her, What makes you passionate? What was the biggest change you have ever undergone? Does this have anything to do with your decision to go to graduate school?

She described in great detail her return to Chile when she was eighteen years old, how she traveled by motorcycle through the countryside and stayed with families in small villages. She talked about the spirit of the country, the compassion of the people, and the poverty in rural areas. When she got back, she decided she wanted to study sustainable technology and rural development. Then she said, "I can't write about that, can I?"

Why not?

The golden rule for essays is this: Be yourself. It is easier, it's more authentic, and it's the subject about which you know most. An essay that is offbeat and sincere is better than one that is mechanical and contrived.

Here are some other suggestions.

KEEP IT SIMPLE

You can only cover so much in a one-page essay. If you try to cram in too much, you sacrifice depth. The audience, after reading hundreds of these, is bound to have a short attention span. Remember, one experience can be profound.

BALANCE CREATIVITY WITH RELEVANCE

An essay can be creative without running too far afield. Remember, this is a medical school application. A treatise on the meaning of life may be cathartic for you but borderline irrelevant to your reader. At some point, you need to bring it back to the core questions: Why medicine? Why you?

DIFFERENTIATE YOURSELF

Rather than chronicle long lists of accomplishments or the blow-by-blow details of your research, use the essay to personalize your application. Out of thousands of undergraduates, what makes you different? What makes you human? This is what will stick in the minds of the readers.

BE POSITIVE

A small dose of optimism will get you a long way. Weed out the complaints, the sarcasm, or any piercing commentaries on the medical profession (for now). Think of your application as a camera—now smile.

SHOULD YOU EXPLAIN PROBLEMS WITH YOUR RECORD?

Whether the personal statement is an appropriate place to discuss drawbacks or discrepancies in your record depends on their significance in your life. Should you detail the reasons for a poor grade in physics? Maybe not. But if it took you seven years to finish undergraduate school because you were working twenty hours a week, you may want to discuss this because your employment was an important factor affecting your undergraduate years. Similarly, if you apply to medical school after a ten-year hiatus, you might want to address this in your essay. Some schools provide space to explain these circumstances in the secondary application as well.

SHOULD YOU DISCUSS YOUR SEXUAL ORIENTATION?

For gay and lesbian students, there is always the question, Should I "out" myself in the essay? Usually this comes up in discussing your work or extracurricular experiences. For example, discussing your involvement with a lesbian health project is tantamount to disclosure.

Many schools now have policies that bar discrimination because of sexual orientation. Many more recognize the need for increased sensitivity to sexual orientation in a medical setting and appreciate diversity in the medical school class. Whether to discuss such issues depends on what you feel comfortable with and the relevance to your medical school application. Sexual preference, in and of itself, will not be of paramount interest to an admissions committee.

Getting Down to Writing

Okay, so now you are ready to write your essay: pencils are sharpened, the computer is fired up. How do you get started?

THINK IT OVER
The task of the essay is to write about yourself. Easy, right? You simply write what you know. But what do you really know about yourself?

If you are like most of us, you charge along in life completing tasks, making decisions, getting angry or enthused without always knowing why. And yet, there are reasons for everything you do. Every feeling and action is connected to something more intimate— those very fibers that determine who you are.

To reveal them, you may need to dig a little. The following questions will help you. Write the answers down in a journal or notebook. Don't worry about focusing for now.

What were the ten most memorable experiences of your life? What were the positive and negative aspects of these experiences? How did these experiences influence you? What did you discover? Did any of these experiences affect your decision to become a physician?

MAKE A BLUEPRINT
Stephen Covey, in *The Seven Habits of Highly Effective People,* emphasizes that "there's a mental or first creation, and a physical or second creation to all things." A carpenter makes a blueprint. An artist does a sketch. Both, before they begin the real work, have "the end in mind."

Before you start writing the essay, think of its goal. If you keep a journal, look it over. Ask yourself, What is it I want to convey about myself? What decisions were most important to my life? What experiences best reflect me?

Once you have an idea of what you want to accomplish with your essay, you can begin writing. For the first draft, try to write without stopping. Let the ideas flow. Don't read it over until you are completely done writing.

WHAT IF YOU HAVE WRITER'S BLOCK?
If you spend more time staring at your screen than writing, try a few of our personal remedies for writer's block:

- Get away from it for a while. Take a walk. Or don't even think about your essay for a week—give your mind a chance to rejuvenate.
- Begin again. Sometimes we get stuck on certain ideas and are too stubborn to give them up, long after we have lost our perspective. Don't try to walk on the wrong foot twice. Take a step back. Think again about your objective. Does the material you are using fit with the "end in mind"?
- Look for meaning. Try to forget the prose and mechanics for a while. Imagine if every time you spoke with a friend, you were concentrating on the pronunciation of your words or the syntax of your sentences. Something would be lost, wouldn't it? Writing, like speaking, is a medium for communicating. If you hyperanalyze the medium, you lose the substance.
- Talk it out. When all efforts are fruitless, appeal to a friend. It's as easy as "Look, what I am trying to say is. . . ." You may also try recording your ideas on a tape recorder. Talking with someone (or yourself) forces upon you the imperative to communicate. Again, it grounds you in the intent.

THE FINAL TOUCHES
Perfect writing is rarely born in one smooth stroke. It is more often what is left over after the windfall of ideas has settled. It is the offshoot of crumpled first drafts, what has bounced off others and returned as new insights, and a never-ending stream of rewrites that ends when you finally declare, Enough!

The point is, the essay is not finished when you give it a once-over and think "not bad." It can always be better.

After you complete the rough draft, read it for overall impression. Does it convey what you originally intended? Are you satisfied with what it says about you? Give it to a friend and ask if it gives the reader an accurate, full picture of you.

Once you are happy with the feel of the essay, you can examine the mechanics and finer details of writing. Look at each sentence individually for meaning. Ask yourself, Does this sentence express what I want to say? Is there a better way to express the same idea? Most schools have tutoring services that will help you to edit your work.

The final run-through is for appearance. Think of the three greatest tenors in the world appearing before millions in anything less than tuxedos. You do not want the thoughtfulness of your essay encased in grammatical errors.

After the essay is completed, give it to a few of your professors to read. Ask them for a no-holds-barred appraisal. What is the impression they get from the essay about you as a person and as a student? You may decide to go back and edit some more or stick with what you have. The most important test is, Do *you* feel comfortable with your essay?

A NOTE ABOUT SECONDARY ESSAYS
Typically, the essay for the secondary application calls for more focused answers. You should be clear and honest about your reasons for applying to a certain school and how your interests are consistent with the school's mission. Vagueness at this point is an indication of lack of direction on your part.

Letters of Recommendation

Student-faculty interaction is a critical part of education. The best students are seen as those who are eager to approach faculty and to develop relationships in which out-of-class learning takes place. These same students will reach out and cultivate relationships in other areas: in volunteer settings, at work, and in the community.

For students at small universities or for the more outgoing student, such interaction comes naturally. Others remain anonymous at the back of a large lecture hall, and getting letters of recommendation is a chore for them.

Reach out to your professors early in your undergraduate years. Get to know your pre-medical advisor so that you are more than just a face. This is not currying favor—it has true benefits for both sides. Most professors enjoy mentoring students and helping them achieve their goals, and writing a letter of recommendation is one way they can do this.

HOW ARE THE LETTERS USED IN THE ADMISSIONS PROCESS?

Along with the interview, letters of recommendation provide key insight into you as seen by others. They are testimony to how well you get along with people, your academic potential, and your activities in the past few years. After other records have proved you a good student, the letters of recommendation indicate whether you have the qualities that would make you a good physician—things like leadership, integrity, self-awareness, and a nimble mind.

WHAT TYPE OF LETTER IS MOST USEFUL?

It is best to get letters from people who have seen you in different settings: your research mentor, a sociology professor, the physician you worked under for a summer project. Your letters do not all have to come from an academic setting. An employer or supervisor of volunteer work may know you better.

Schools usually request three to five letters of recommendation. Often, they specify the type of letter. For example, a school may require one evaluation from a science professor and one from a professor in another discipline. Many osteopathic schools want a letter of recommendation from an osteopathic physician. To be safe, you should plan to get an assortment of letters.

Letters of recommendation that reiterate what is evident from your transcripts ("Maria received an A in my physics class") or are vague ("Ray is a fine candidate") are not useful. Letters should focus on specific qualities, particularly as they relate to medicine.

If you have faced certain hardships, you may ask someone with insight into your experience to write a letter. This person may shed light on personal strengths such as perseverance and self-motivation, and provide context to your accomplishments.

PROTOCOL WHEN REQUESTING THE LETTERS

Schedule a meeting with the person you are asking to recommend you. Explain your plans and ask if she or he would feel comfortable writing a letter of recommendation for you. If the person seems at all hesitant, you should seek someone else. Another approach for the shy or uncertain student is to ask the person for advice about getting a letter of recommendation and see if the person volunteers.

If you do not know the person well, you should provide a résumé along with a description of your background, your interests and activities. In fact, do this for all your references so that they can select rather than recall the most important information about you. Let them know the date the letter needs to be sent, and provide all the necessary materials and addresses.

A little guidance makes it easier on the people writing your letters. If necessary, explain how admissions committees use recommendation letters and what type of information is most useful, and highlight specific qualities you think they might mention about you.

Many schools have a file service for letters of recommendation. Commonly, a pre-medical committee writes a composite letter of recommendation based on individual letters or an interview. Most medical schools require the composite letter when a pre-medical committee exists at the school. Schools also prefer that letters of recommendation remain confidential.

WHEN TO START GATHERING THE LETTERS

You may begin asking for letters of recommendation as early as the end of sophomore year. Don't wait until a few months before applications are due. If you want a thoughtful letter, you have to give the person sufficient time—at least four to six weeks. Otherwise you are in the awkward position of hassling the professor, and worrying about whether the letter is going to get done in time.

The Final Word: Be Proactive

It's easy during all the activity that accompanies this stage of the application process to become lost, discouraged, or disempowered. You'll have a stream of deadlines and demands in a structured process as well as the strain of not knowing, having your ego twisted and pulled, and confronting the ever-uncertain envelope.

The process is tough—no doubt. It's also, in some ways, rigid and uncompromising. But you needn't feel confined, either in spirit or in action, by the structure. Between applications, instead of running to the mailbox, do something proactive: re-read the catalogs, visit schools, call students, make an appointment with a professor. Use this time to pay closer attention to details and to think about your pending decision of where to attend medical school. Between the time of your primary and secondary applications, you might want to make another longer visit to one or more of your first-choice schools to help you with your final decision (this also helps you gather more information for your secondary essay).

After you complete your secondaries, you have a while for a short rest—but not too long. You are about to begin the most busy (and exciting) phase of the admissions process: the interview.

12

THE INTERVIEW

Nothing quite equals the anticipation and excitement of preparing for an interview that will inordinately affect your life. This is particularly true for pre-medical students as the day of the medical school interview approaches.

I remember daydreaming about this event in my first year as a pre-medical student. While my chemistry professor discussed the importance of electronegativity to intermolecular bonding, I lost myself in my first medical school interview. I envisioned myself sitting silently on a black stool as a panel of ten physicians in grey suits assembled behind a large conference table. The man in the middle directed the first of a series of grueling questions at me while his colleagues scrutinized my every move. I felt my face warm over and I began to stammer.

Hours later, I saw myself—the final product—a pathetic beet-faced interviewee sunken down on her little black stool spitting out an endless stream of clichés. The panel of physicians folded up their briefcases, shook their heads, and then, in a unified voice descending upon me, repeated, "We're sorry, Miss, it's over . . . it's over . . . it's over. . . ." Then came a jolt from the side: "Jen, wake up, it's over. The lecture is over."

Over the years, these fantasies took a new shape, at first reasonable and then grandiose. En route to the university, I imagined myself discussing thoughtfully my relationship with my family. In line at the bank, I outlined the most pressing problems in our national health care system. On the way to class, I gave an impassioned speech on the need for more humane medical education.

These fantasies helped ease my anxiety by allowing me to define, if only in my mind, what to expect from the interview. As with so much else in the medical school application process, it wasn't the interview itself that caused my anxiety. It was the uncertainty that characterized this event. As scary as it is, we can tackle the MCAT if we know what material it is going to cover. But what will the interview cover? If we have no idea what it is about, we have no way of preparing for it.

It's not as if no one discusses The Interview. Quite the opposite. At any university where there are many pre-medical students, there will be considerable talk about this topic. Unfortunately, most of what you hear is based on personal stories and has little grounding in fact.

About the role of the interview in the admissions committee's decision, everyone has an opinion. Some applicants contend that the interview is the most important factor in the admissions process. Right before my first interview, an older and seemingly wiser student had this advice: "If you do well, you're in. If you mess up, it's all over." Other students claim that the interview is insignificant, except as a tool to weed out the bad apples (people considered for one reason or another unsuitable for the profession).

About the interview itself, the stories are equally diverse. Most applicants, however, concede that the interview experience is really the luck of the draw. It depends on the interviewer, the school, and of course, you. Keeping this in mind, you should know that there is no prescribed code of behavior for interviews. You can, however, prepare yourself to handle the circumstances that come your way if you know the facts about the process beforehand.

THE ROLE OF THE INTERVIEW IN THE SELECTION PROCESS

Medical schools use the interview to measure personal qualities that are important for a career in medicine, yet not easily measured in the formal application materials. The interview also is an essential recruitment tool. It gives a school the opportunity to portray itself in the best possible light, thus encouraging you to attend should you be accepted.

Most schools consider the interview (along with letters of recommendation) to be the third most important factor for admission, after your GPA and MCAT scores. Unfortunately, not everyone gets the benefit of having an interview. On average, schools grant interviews to only 15–20 percent of the applicant pool. If you make it to this stage, you are among the top candidates competing for a spot in the class. In fact, some schools consider all candidates at this point to be on an equal footing.

The interview provides additional insight into your personal qualities, communication skills, and personal rapport. It is useful for identifying applicants at either end of the personality spectrum: those who possess outstanding personal qualities and social skills and those who may have significant character flaws. For these applicants, the interview may well be the salient factor in the committee's decision.

All applicants must pass through the interview process, even students with perfect grades and top MCAT scores. In fact, extremely ambitious types and high achievers may attract especially rigorous scrutiny. Schools of medicine want students who can master their curriculum, but not at the expense of essential social skills or personal maturity. Therefore, a strong interview may place an applicant with a "good enough" academic record in a better position than that of a valedictorian who is emotionally immature.

WHAT THE INTERVIEW CAN DO FOR YOU

The interview exists not simply to judge you, the eager and defenseless applicant. It is also a chance for you to judge the school. Your interview experience will contribute to your decision about what school is best for you. This is an important point for you to remember, as it may help to take some pressure off during the interview.

The day of the interview may be your first real-life encounter with the school. This is your opportunity to interact with students and faculty and see firsthand the services and facilities the university has to offer. It's a time to wander about, to gain a sense of the school environment and the city in which you could potentially be living, working, and studying for the next four or more years of your life.

If at any point you were having problems distinguishing one medical school from the next, your interviews will convince you of the uniqueness of each medical school. As you visit more schools, you will learn about the qualities of a program that will make a difference in your life as a medical student. You will refine the list of what is most important to you—whether that be the curriculum, the student community, or the city itself.

INTERVIEW POLICIES AND PROCEDURES

Most schools require you to have at least one interview, more commonly two. The interview usually lasts a half hour to an hour and may be with any one of the members of the admissions committee (faculty, physicians, medical students, or alumni). It is usually one-on-one, although a few schools may conduct group interviews or have more than one interviewer present. Most often, you will not know the name of your interviewer until the day of your interview. Presumably, this prevents students from seeking personal information about this person beforehand. Many schools arrange a formal interview day with a schedule of activities for a group of applicants. If this is the case, they expect you to arrive early in the morning and stay into the afternoon. In addition to your interviews, the day's activities may include a tour of the school, a group meeting with a representative from the financial aid office, a question-and-answer session with current students, or the option of attending some classes. Other schools arrange only for your interviews, and the rest of the time you are on your own.

Three Types of Interviews

Each school has a particular policy regarding the amount of knowledge the interviewer has about you ahead of time. The most common types of interviews are the following.

THE OPEN INTERVIEW
In this type of interview, the interviewer has full access to your file before you meet. The interviewer receives your file about a week before the interview and uses these materials to gain background information on you. This allows her or him to introduce relevant topics and to clarify issues on your record if need be.

THE BLIND INTERVIEW
In this approach, the interviewer knows your name and nothing else. This is a rather unorthodox format, just starting to catch on. The

schools that use this method are trying to avoid any bias that the interviewer may have based on your application materials. With this method, the basis for your evaluation will come solely from your hour of personal interaction.

Some applicants are uneasy with this method. The interview often begins with, "So, tell me about yourself," a task that can be both time-consuming and difficult. However, it also creates a less rigid environment, which could be favorable if you relate better this way.

THE SEMIBLIND INTERVIEW

In this type of interview, the interviewer does not have access to your file. Rather, the interviewer is given a sheet of paper that you fill out before the interview, containing your educational background and personal interests. This provides some direction for the interview but reduces the bias that can result when the interviewer is privy to your entire file.

Get the Interview Details Ahead of Time

You should find out about a school's interview policies and procedures ahead of time. Following are some questions you will want to answer:

- How many applicants were or will be granted interviews?
- How many offers of admission does the school typically make to fill how many spots in next year's class?
- How many interviews will you have? Will these be with faculty members, physicians at the school of medicine, medical students, or a combination?
- Is it a blind or semiblind interview, or does the interviewer have access to your file?
- What arrangements for overnight lodging exist?
- Will there be a tour? Will you have the opportunity to attend classes?

Answers to most of these questions can be found in your application materials, the school catalog, or a current edition of *Medical School Admission Requirements* (MSAR). What you can't find out from those sources, you should ask the admissions office directly.

PREPARATION FOR THE INTERVIEW

By late fall or winter, you should have completed most of your secondary applications and be ready for the interview process. Getting ready for the medical school interview requires more than booking a flight and showing up at the school. There are other factors to consider.

Cost and Time Commitment

The interview is the most expensive part of applying to medical school. Transportation costs, lodging and food, and possible lost wages from work can add up if you have many interviews at different times in different places. A survey by the Association of American Medical Colleges (AAMC) indicates that applicants spend an average of four hundred dollars on interviews.

Time is also a factor. Interviewing for medical school requires some adjustments in your work and school schedule. In the same survey, 40 percent of students reported missing fifteen or more days for the application process. Depending on how many interviews you have, you may need to reduce other commitments.

When a school invites you for an interview, you will be asked when you are available. From these options, the school schedules you for a specific date. If you will be in the area for an interview at another school, the schools will do their best to work with you. If you have time restrictions or a problem with your interview date, call and explain your circumstances. I have heard of schools that granted interviews before the formal interview process began, on a weekend, or even over dinner when there were extenuating circumstances.

Personal Appearance

Beyond making sure your shoes are shined and nails clipped and clean, what are the dos and don'ts of dressing for the interview?

At the first interview day I attended, everyone might as well have been dressed for a funeral. The women were in black suits with white shirts, the men in grey suits and conservative ties. My first thought was that they all had read the same book on proper interview etiquette or had heeded the advice of counselors who played it safe with a prescribed dress code for all applicants.

Admittedly, conventional dress is best for the interview. You are better off appearing as a drone than sticking out as the only applicant with a high-fashion suit and electric blue flowered tie, or a hot pink skirt and matching heels. In a perfectly unbiased interview process, it wouldn't matter one iota, but we all know that in real life it does. In fact, social science research suggests that people make lasting impressions based on the first few minutes of contact. In that brief time, you want to draw attention to your personality rather than to your attire.

Does that mean a classic black/navy/grey suit and white shirt are essential? Should men cut their hair (including beards and mustaches)? Should women reduce their makeup and jewelry (or include some, if they normally don't use them)? Not necessarily. It is best to be yourself and present yourself as you feel comfortable. However, you have to remember with whom you are meeting and what your interviewer's frame of mind will be.

A phenomenon called the similarity hypothesis has been documented by behavioral scientists. It states, quite simply, that a person is more comfortable with people who seem to look, think, and act like him or her.

Now imagine a convention of female and male academic physicians. What are they wearing? Don't deviate too far from that image. To the physicians who conduct your interview, you are the next generation of them. Logically, then, they assume you will look like them. Be yourself, but remember that there may only be a half hour for an interviewer to formulate an opinion of you that could deeply affect your life.

Mental Readiness

Obviously, much more time and effort are required for mental preparation than for physical appearance. To prepare for the medical school interview, you will need to become informed about current health care issues and do some self-reflection. These tips will get you started.

- Verse yourself on health care issues, problems facing the medical profession, and personal dilemmas confronted by physicians. A good source of information from the medical perspective is current journals or newsletters, including the *American Medical*

Association News, Journal of the American Medical Association, Academic Medicine Journal, and *New England Journal of Medicine.* Be prepared to put forth some personal perspectives on the issues.

- Research the school to which you are applying. You should be able to articulate exactly why you are applying to that particular school. What appeals to you about the curriculum, the hospitals, and the location?
- Think about the experiences that you have had in your life, particularly those related to the medical field. Ask yourself why you did what you did, what you learned from the experiences, and how they affected you and your career goals. Be able to explain the motivation behind your actions, and your reactions to the outcomes.
- Think about the setbacks that you have had in your life. How did you overcome them? What did they teach you about yourself?
- Think about the people who have had the greatest influence on you. What did you admire in them? In what way did they help you?
- Think about the areas of medicine that interest you the most. What sparks your interest? What personal assets do you have that are compatible with these areas?

Getting There and Getting Settled

Give yourself enough time to get to the school and compose yourself. If the school is out of state, you should plan to arrive the night before. Most schools will enclose a list of inexpensive housing in the area. If it is available, staying with a medical student for a night is an excellent opportunity to get the inside scoop on the school, to have last-minute questions answered, and to get tips about the interviewing process. On the other hand, staying with a medical student the night before your interview may be emotionally taxing, a high-energy activity. For some people, it is important to have some time alone, to collect their thoughts and be comfortable before their interview day.

Most schools will ask you to report to the admissions office on the day of your interview. At that time, they will give you details about the time and place of your interview and a schedule of the day's activities (if this applies). It is rare not to encounter other interviewees milling around the office, probably just as bewildered and nervous as you are. Take advantage of this situation to diffuse the anxiety. Find out where they've interviewed. What were their impressions of these schools? Why are they applying to this school? By sharing experiences you will feel more relaxed with yourself and the people around you. Remember, you're all in this together.

THE INTERVIEW HOUR

Usually, you will meet your interviewer at his or her office. Some of these places can be quite hard to find, so give yourself enough time to get there. For example, one of my interviews was at a temporary research site—a bunch of trailers down a dirt road over the railroad tracks. Plan on getting there about a half hour ahead of time. The best first impression you can make is to be waiting when your interviewer arrives.

Interviews do not always begin and end on time as planned. Faculty members at a school of medicine are on extremely tight schedules and cram interviews between classes, appointments with patients, or even surgery. If your interview begins late, is interrupted, or ends short, give them the benefit of the doubt and be patient.

While waiting for your interview, take a deep breath, relax, and be satisfied with yourself and what you know. There is no use trying to speed-read the school catalog for more information or play back rehearsed answers to hypothetical questions. Think of it this way: what subject do you know more about than yourself? This should give you more than enough room to feel comfortable—you are the expert.

Be Yourself

Everybody goes into the interview with some fears, either that they will not know the "right" answers or that they will not be able to express their ideas clearly. Don't stress yourself out on this. Nobody blows an interview with one imperfect response. Besides, the objective of the interview is not to be perfect. Those who approach it with that intent may come off as self-aggrandizing and arrogant (not good qualities for a future physician).

Even more important than your accomplishments or the articulation of your ideas are your personal maturity and self-awareness. Can you recognize your strengths as well as your weaknesses? Are you able to speak honestly about your achievements as well as the difficult experiences?

The interview should provide insight into you—the reasons why you started a certain project, the mistakes you made and what you learned from them, and how your life experiences have led to your decision to become a doctor or to apply to that particular school. This interpretation of your experience is the missing link in your academic transcript and the list of activities in your file. It adds continuity and personal meaning to an application that is otherwise two-dimensional. It also helps the interviewer understand the circumstances behind any potential drawbacks or ambiguities on your record.

Don't glaze over the difficult experiences that you have had, especially if they are reflected in your application (for instance, a semester off from school). Every one of us, including esteemed faculty and physicians and deans of medical schools, have been through our share of tough times. No one expects—nor is it desired—that your path to the doors of medical school has always been rosy. It is these personal struggles that deepen character. Instead of dwelling on your hardships or excusing your mistakes, focus on what you learned from your experiences.

Keep a positive outlook about yourself. As an actress friend said to me, "Life is the only theater where the rehearsal is also the final production." For your achievements as well as your follies, be proud of what you have created.

Finally, be an active participant in the interview. You are not there to be interrogated. Nor are you a one-person show. Think of the interview as a conversation between friends (or at least colleagues). Relax. Wait for an exchange. Get a sense of the other person. This makes for more meaningful interaction.

Despite your efforts, some interviews will remain formal to the end, never budging off the topic of health care or medical education. Others will break down into loose conversation within a matter of minutes, passing through jokes and into philosophical debate. The key is to be aware at all times. Don't be afraid to deviate from the topic a bit, but recognize how far you can go with any one interviewer.

How to Respond to Difficult Questions

The horror stories you may have heard about some interviews can heighten your anxiety. We have all heard about the interviewers who dwell on supercontroversial issues (abortion, gay and lesbian rights, euthanasia) or blast you with superknowledge questions (politics, health care reform, history, medical information, statistics) or even raise the dreaded "common knowledge" questions (current affairs, classic art and literature, prominent people) or who are simply boorish and inappropriate.

The way you respond to a difficult question often tells more about you as a person than your actual response. For example, if you feel ill-prepared to answer a question, do you try to muster something up? Do you freak out? Or do you tell them genuinely that you cannot answer the question?

CONTROVERSIAL ISSUES

If your interviewer asks you to take a side on a controversial issue, offer your honest opinion. Even if you run into an ideological conflict, it is unlikely that your interviewer will perceive you negatively as a result. If you try to skirt the issue, or have no opinion at all, you give the impression of someone who is either duplicitous or uninformed.

As a doctor, you will frequently confront controversial issues and ethical dilemmas. It is most important that you be forthright and able to articulate your ideas clearly.

WHEN PERSONALITIES CLASH

There is a chance that you may find yourself at odds with your interviewer. The best policy here is to practice temperance. It may be that you consider the interviewer reprehensible as a person, that his or her political views or way of life are different from yours. You must, however, remember why you are there. The interview is a place for exchange, not arguments. If an interviewer makes a statement or asks you a question that you feel is offensive or inappropriate, deal with it calmly and then report the issue to higher-ups at the school of medicine later.

I remember three such occasions. One interviewer used blatantly racist language. Another talked to me nonstop about the "big bucks" doctors can make in the right specialty. And another, a medical student, baited me about affirmative action, asking me to give examples supporting his view on the matter (I was of the opposite opinion). Undoubtedly, these interactions affected my impression of the school. Fortunately, I had other, supportive interviewers who helped me keep my perspective on the school as a whole when deciding where to attend.

Almost every applicant can expect one or two uncomfortable experiences. A recent study at one medical school indicated that women are asked about their plans for having children significantly more often than men. Huong recalls one interviewer who responded to her life story (emigrating to the United States after her mother's death) with, "Well that's not so unique, we have many Vietnamese here." For her, this insensitivity was enough to make her reconsider what had been her first-choice school.

On the other hand, certain comments warrant a more lighthearted approach. Anita chuckles at some of the questions she was asked:

> One interviewer wanted to know if I was going into medicine for the money. I laughed and said, "You have to be kidding. Do you know how much money it cost me to leave investment banking and go to medical school?" Another asked me how much money I made as an investment banker. I said, "I will tell you that if you tell me how much you make as a physician."

HOW MUCH DO YOU KNOW?

Regarding questions that test you on specific points of knowledge, we make one recommendation. Talk about the things you know, and don't pretend you know things that you don't.

I learned this lesson while interviewing at my first-choice school. The woman interviewing me began explaining the awe that she felt for Madame Curie, the scientist who discovered radium while raising several children and who subsequently became the first person to win two Nobel prizes. While my interviewer talked about how Madame Curie had served as a source of inspiration for her and women in medicine throughout the world, I tried desperately to recall who this wonder woman was. I remember the apprehension of that moment— should I pretend I knew who Madame Curie was, or admit my ignorance up front? Fearing a question on the subject later (e.g., How would you compare your life with that of Madame Curie?), I opted for the latter. I looked the interviewer in the face and said, "Who is that?"

This experience did not go without reproach. I called my parents long-distance after the interview. They were horrified. "How on earth could you study chemistry, want to be a doctor, and not have heard of Madame Curie?" asked my mother. "The woman is discussing her life-long idol, and you interrupt her with 'who's that?'" my father chimed in on the other line. "Couldn't you have just nodded your head silently in agreement?"

I obsessed on this blunder for days. After asking several of my friends, it seemed that everyone really did know who Madame Curie was. This was a double whammy. Not only was I ignorant of such a celebrated woman, I had admitted my ignorance.

In retrospect, I would react the same way again. And I recommend that you do the same. The interview is not a place to dazzle them with the infallibility of your intelligence or knowledge. It is primarily an opportunity to provide a glimpse of you—the real thing. So if you do not know something, forget it and go on. Chances are, if you don't become flustered, they won't even remember it. In my case, it didn't make such a difference. Three weeks later, I received a letter of acceptance from this school.

As demonstrated by this example, it can be disputed whether a question tests the finer points of knowledge or is something that would be considered "common knowledge" to most people. Your interviewer may overlook the fact that you don't know the percentage of people in the United States infected with the HIV virus (a question posed to me) or the difference between glucose and sucrose (a question posed to a friend). However, you'd be in a real uncomfortable position if you didn't know the name of the governor of your own state. Excusing yourself would be even more absurd, as a student in that situation did, explaining his lack of basic political information with, "I'm not much for politics; much too busy with school."

To practice as a competent physician today, a person must be able to understand medicine as it relates to many different systems, including politics, economics, current affairs, and diverse cultural systems. Medical schools are looking for applicants who have this general knowledge base. If you do not consider yourself well versed in these matters, it is something you should try to improve, not because of the interview but as a step on the path toward becoming an informed and responsible physician.

Ending the Interview

By the end of the interview, you should have a feel for how receptive your interviewer is and what types of issues can be raised. You might pose questions that your interviewer would have insight into. For example, if you are a woman interviewing with a woman physician, you might want to know if she has a family, how she copes with multiple role responsibilities and other gender-specific issues. You should avoid questions that you can answer from the school catalog or that pertain to your application.

When leaving the interview, thank the interviewer for her or his time, using the full name with appropriate title. As soon as possible (preferably the next day), write a brief thank-you note. Mentioning anything about your application or chances of getting in is inappropriate. Simply express thanks, and if the interviewer was helpful in certain ways, say so.

MAKING THE MOST OF YOUR INTERVIEW DAY

The medical school will design most interview days to maximize your exposure to the school's facilities, services, and environment. Attending tours and classes and speaking with students should give you much of the information you need, but don't let that stop you from exploring on your own. Take it upon yourself to personalize the process. Dream up ways that will give you a closer and different feel for the school, and then take the initiative. Here are some ideas:

- Find out what student organizations exist. Attend a meeting of one in which you are interested.
- If you have an area of particular interest, clinical or research, call a professor in that field and ask if you could meet briefly with her or him. Many faculty members would be flattered to be ap-

proached in this way. Be sure you make an appointment ahead of time.

- Arrange to meet with a student or two with the same interests or background as you. Find out why they chose this school and if it has lived up to their expectations. Ask them about the negative aspects of the school.
- Go to the place where most students congregate (student lounges). Watch what is going on. Do students seem to be part of a tight-knit community, or are they aloof? Are they discussing shared classes or activities outside of school?
- Check out the bulletin boards in and around crowded areas. What types of notices are there (announcements for club meetings, fellowships for minorities, courses on popular health in Central America, political rallies, a get-together at a professor's house)?
- Attend a few classes. Watch how students interact before and after class. What is the professor's relationship with the students? Do most students attend class? Do the students ask questions during a lecture and afterward?

Remember to take notes on what you learn during the day of the interview. Take down addresses of people you meet. They can be helpful later if you have additional questions or simply need advice. Besides, it is never too early to establish contacts with people who have interests similar to yours.

A short while after the interview, you will make a number of important choices about your career and your future. By getting yourself prepared—mentally, physically, and otherwise—you can make the interview process work for you.

13

MAKING THE TRANSITION TO MEDICAL SCHOOL

with Peter Muennig, M.D.

At last, you have reached the point you worked and planned for all these years: You are a medical student. But are you prepared for what lies in store?

Making the actual transition to medical school is a move that involves almost every aspect of your life. You will be faced with many challenges—settling into a different city, rebuilding your social network, assuming the responsibilities of a medical student, and adjusting to a new academic environment. No matter how well you prepare, there will be a number of surprises and glitches that will come to alter even your best-laid plans.

Do not fear! The transition to medical school is not meant to be easy. This is for a reason. While it may at times be overwhelming, this transition offers you the possibility for amazing personal and academic growth. In the uncertainty of confronting your new environment you will be called to confront yourself, to thoughtfully reconsider who you are and what you are doing.

This is the hallmark of making a positive transition, when you meet the challenges of a new environment or situation and discover yourself to be something more than you were when you first began. This is our hope for you. Although it is impossible to anticipate all the challenges ahead, we offer some advice to arm you in the battle against being overwhelmed and to allow you to make the most of the next few years.

FINDING A HOME

The first step to happiness in medical school is finding the right place to live. This is where you will eat, sleep, study, and hang out for the next year or so. If you appreciate the arts, find a place in an artistic community. If you need sunshine, look for an apartment with lots of windows.

Remember, no matter how balanced you are before you enter medical school, you are bound to feel medical studies taking over your life. Living in a place you call home, in a community that you appreciate, with access to activities that you enjoy, will help you keep a perspective on the world and yourself outside of medicine.

Of course, you also need to maintain a connection within the world of medicine—that is, your classmates. Your classmates will help you manage the logistics of day-to-day life as a medical student, like test tips and exam times and locations (especially when they change). They are the people with whom you will grow tired in the early morning with your head full of study mnemonics, the ones who will best understand your feelings about school, and the people who you will work with in the future.

LEARNING MEDICINE—
WHAT WILL IT BE LIKE?

For most of us, medical school requires dramatic adjustments in the way we viewing learning.

A Lifetime of Learning

As an undergraduate student, you were motivated to learn by grades and what would be covered by tests and exams. Typically, you were confronted with a limited body of information and the end was always in sight. You could cram for the final exam and, at the end of the semester, heave a sigh of relief and throw away all your notes.

For the most part, this is not true of learning medicine. In medicine, you commit yourself to a lifetime of learning. The material that you study for exams is also the basis of your future practice as a physician. As a result, you will need to assume greater personal responsibility for learning.

Cooperative Learning

To encourage a more healthy learning environment, many medical schools have changed to a pass/no pass grading system in the first two years. In this environment, students are more inclined to work together and to share information, ideas, and resources. Rather than competing for grades, students engage in cooperative learning.

Functioning well in this environment requires a unique perspective: the whole process is there for you. Instead of working for the A, you work for your own betterment. It is a more ethereal reward system that is internalized, requiring a good deal of self-confidence and self-initiative.

Managing the Information Overload

The medical sciences encompass a vast and seemingly endless body of knowledge. Many first-year medical students assume that they must conquer this incredible mountain of information. These students feverishly memorize details for their exams and either become overwhelmed in the process or quickly forget everything after the exam.

Learning in medical school is said to be like taking sips from a fire hydrant. The more you take in, the more you realize how much you have yet to learn. This leads to the common first-year medical student complex: "I can't learn it all," "I can't do it," "I shouldn't be here" (the committee must have made a mistake). Not true. You can do it, but it requires a different type of thinking than most undergraduates are accustomed to.

As a medical student, you must develop the ability to distinguish what is *most important* from an overwhelming mass of details. Rather than spending your first year memorizing all the virulence factors of every microorganism, focus on the concepts and principles of what you are reading. Later, when you see the information again (and you will), when it is connected to a patient and to real human suffering, you will learn the pertinent details and you won't forget them.

CONQUERING THE BASIC SCIENCES

An important part of the practice of medicine is understanding the basic sciences. The question is, How much basic science is enough?

Can you get through medical school without knowing about the ocular dominance columns in the hypercolumns of the visual cortex (and still be a good doctor)?

The answer to this question will depend on your professors and, importantly, on who sits on your course curriculum committee. If it's composed primarily of basic science researchers—neuroanatomists, microbiologists, physiologists—you may be inclined to believe that each detailed mechanism (depending on what field they're in) holds the key to the current practice of medicine. If you talk to a clinician who's practicing in the community about some of these scientific details (for example, the ocular dominance columns), you're likely to get a puzzled look (translation: they've never heard of them).

It's up to you to strike a balance between basic science knowledge and clinical relevance. In part, this will depend on your priorities and interests in medicine. If you are interested in surgery, you may find it beneficial to know all the superficial veins in the arm. Otherwise, you may decide only to learn enough detail to pass your anatomy exam, and then concentrate your efforts elsewhere. In the future, if you need to know this information in detail, you can always look it up.

The most vital years of medical school, both in terms of your grades (for residency programs) and actually developing the skills and knowledge to practice medicine, are the clinical years (the wards). Some of the course work that students feel they use most on the wards includes the Introduction to Clinical Medicine course, microbiology, psychiatry, pharmacology, epidemiology, and pathology.

METHODS FOR LEARNING

Lectures

The overwhelming majority of medical schools are lecture-based in the first two years. These schools may provide up to thirty hours of basic science lectures per week. How often you choose to attend lectures will depend on your personal learning style, how valuable you deem these lectures to be, and how much structure you want in your personal and academic life (at some schools, this is a moot point—attendance is mandatory).

Many students learn best through verbal and visual presentation. These students may appreciate the multimedia aspects of lecture—

listening to someone speak, reviewing slides, or watching a video. Other students are fidgeting in their chairs (or asleep) five minutes into the presentation. These students find that they can learn the same information faster and better on their own (and free up eight hours a day to spend as they please).

Students who choose to forgo the lecture circuit entirely will inevitably miss some inspiring and memorable moments—when the neurologist acts out all the types of seizures in full animation, when you learn of the struggle of Lenin's troops against typhus, or when a seven-year-old child with Down syndrome breaks into song.

Each student will need to develop his or her own approach to lectures—attend lectures for a certain class, select for the best professors, or follow your mood at the moment (a hit-or-miss approach). Talk with students in the class before yours to find out which classes and professors made an impression on them. Go to the first few lectures of each class to see which professors will keep you awake. Or look over the syllabus ahead of time and earmark those topics you find most appealing.

Studying

Regardless of whether you are faithfully present at each lecture or only show up for exams, you will study a lot. You have several resources for studying: lecture notes, tutorial groups and courses, textbooks and journals, and your classmates.

LECTURE NOTES
Your primary resource should be your lecture notes. In almost any course, if you know and understand your lecture notes (or the ones you bought from a note-taking service), you will do well in that course. Most schools have note-taking services. Some use a system of cooperative note taking, in which students alternate taking notes and share them with each other. Other schools provide syllabi for each course with a composite of notes written by each lecturer.

TUTORIAL GROUPS AND COURSES
Some schools offer tutorial courses, which can be an excellent way to brush up on material and to reinforce what you have learned in lecture. Many schools also offer computer-assisted instruction, videos, or other simulated exercises to aid the learning process.

TEXTBOOKS

During your pre-clinical years you will probably use a laboratory textbook, a microbiology or pharmacology textbook, and occasionally a pathology text. Otherwise, you should avoid the bookstore for the first two years. Most medical texts inundate you with detail and are not appropriate for the needs of most medical students.

If you really want a textbook, most schools keep a selection of medical books on reserve at the library. This is a great resource if you want more in-depth discussion of a subject or if a course is so confusing that you need an additional source from which to learn.

JOURNALS

You are now forging your way ahead with great efficiency, so reward yourself with a subscription to your favorite medical journal. Subscriptions are available for students at reduced rates. The *New England Journal of Medicine* is a great supplement to your education. You can also delve into specialty journals that interest you. These journals will keep you up-to-date on areas of interest, expose you to current issues in medicine, and get you into the habit of reading research articles. Reading journals will also help you immeasurably on the wards when you do your clinical work.

YOUR CLASSMATES

When it comes to learning medicine, your classmates are indispensable. Ideally they are a source of support and of inspired learning. They will fill you in when you miss a lecture, help to clarify points of misunderstanding, and share other student responsibilities. Studying with a friend may be more stimulating and effective than falling asleep over a pile of dry lecture notes.

STAYING WHOLE

Your goal in attending medical school is to educate yourself to become a physician and simultaneously grow as a person. At times, the two tasks may seem incompatible. What you need as a person may not be fulfilled in the quick pause between exams. In turn, what is expected of you as a student may at times infringe upon deeper values that you hold and upon ideas about the way that you wish to live your life. Each of us, no matter how gung ho we are about medicine, how rigged up we are to be a good student, how optimistic or grounded we are as people, may experience this schism. In the tug-of-war between our new role as young doctors and the more fundamental aspects of our being, several feelings may emerge: frustration with ourselves and the profession, self-doubt, or anger.

These feelings, while very common, are often not addressed as part of the medical school experience. Worse, they exist on the fringes, are denied, or are deliberately suppressed by students in an attempt to survive, to make it past the next exam, to not fall in disfavor with the institution, or to not be perceived as weak by classmates.

This is not the approach that you should take, not if your goal is to grow as a person. These feelings are a sign of a fracture that needs to be addressed. If you try to mask them, you will lose the benefit of learning that any difficult experience offers. Instead, you should try to understand what is happening, to work through it, and ultimately to heal the fracture. That way, when you come out of the process of medical school, you are somehow different, but you are also somehow more insightful about yourself, true to who you want to be, and closer to whole.

In case this sounds too nebulous to be practical, we now examine some real situations where this approach will help you.

Keeping Tabs on Your Emotional Well-Being

It's no secret that medical school can be extremely stressful. At times, you may find yourself wishing that you had taken a year off. You may even have doubts about your decision to enter medicine.

Each of us manages stress in her or his own way. Some people seek a creative outlet, for example, by writing and reading poetry. Others find release through a jog in the park. Family and friends may provide emotional support or a safe place to blow off steam. It may help you to learn stress reduction techniques or better time management. For more advice on stress management, see Chapter 7.

Research shows that medical students are at greater risk for depression than persons of the same age in the general population. Be aware of the warning signs: feelings of worthlessness or guilt, a weight change, or problems sleeping. If this happens to you (or a friend), seek help.

Initially, the best place to go for personal problems is the Counseling Center or psychological services on campus. All counseling is confidential and is usually free for students. In addition, many nonprofit organizations, such as Planned Parenthood, Jewish Social Services, or Family Services Foundation, offer free or discounted counseling services. Your primary care physician at the Health Center can probably refer you to these services.

Academic Expectations

For students who have always excelled in academics, the pressure to keep up a high level of academic achievement can be immense. No one wants the stigma of being the struggling student, the one who falls through the cracks, who can't make it in medical school.

And yet, the reality is that many students have difficulty adapting to the fast pace and style of learning in medical school. I can still remember the tension in the air as my classmates and I stood in groups of four around the cadavers for our first anatomy exam. Later that week, I heaved a sigh of relief to find a passing grade matched to my ID number on the list of test results. What I didn't expect was to find myself a few hours later holding my best friend as she cried because she was one of the three students who failed.

It is common to confront feelings of self-doubt about your ability—that you aren't cut out to be a doctor; you aren't smart enough; or you should have done better on an exam. Recognizing that you don't sit on top of the world, or that you can't always glide through academics is a humbling experience. This can also be a positive experience if you are able to learn a lesson from the experience of your own limitations and if it inspires you to work harder, to push yourself. Or it can be catastrophic, if it manifests itself as inadequacy or self-denigration.

Surviving the medical school experience with your academic ego intact requires that you develop your own standards of personal and academic achievement. We all know what is expected of us by our professors and the administration, but we should be cautious not to use these standards as the sole measure of our achievement. Exams are at best a mediocre determination of how well you are assuming the skills that will make you a good physician. Other immeasurable qualities are just as important.

If you are having academic difficulty, you shouldn't deny the situation. Have enough faith in yourself to get the help you need and not to delay (it only gets worse). As in undergraduate education, your professor is the number-one resource for advice on how to approach the material most effectively. Many schools also have tutoring centers for students needing help in certain areas.

Surviving the Wards

On the wards, you will assume the role of a doctor in training. Your responsibilities include the more routine activities of a doctor—writing a History and Physical, "prerounding" on patients (arriving early in the hospital to check events overnight before team rounds), and presenting cases to other doctors at various levels of training—interns, residents, and attending physicians.

The task of a medical student in the clinical years, as one medical educator put it, is to be a chameleon. You must learn to function just as well in a competitive, highly academic, tertiary care center as you would in a laid-back community clinic. You should appear just as comfortable with the surgeons as you do with the psychiatrists or the pediatricians.

To act like a chameleon is a necessary tactic for survival. Unfortunately, the demands of adapting to your environments may also threaten your sense of self if you don't have a means of connecting with yourself during the process. The secret is to recognize what you can learn from the environment and from others while remaining true to your deeper beliefs and values.

Maneuvering in the Medical Hierarchy

When you are in medical school, you will possibly run into sticky situations concerning the medical hierarchy. Your nemeses may include professors, impossible residents (doctors just out of medical school training for a specialty), or attendings (doctors in practice). Furthermore, these people will be writing your evaluations.

If it's simply a case of conflicting personalities, the most reasonable approach is to try to get along. This is particularly important if you have to spend a lot of time with this person. Try to understand where the person is coming from and how you can adapt yourself to make it easier. If there is a point of contention, challenge the person gently. Remember that you are entering a profession where tact is everything, not only with patients but with your peers and your teachers.

Situations where there is a question of inappropriate or unethical behavior require deeper consideration. Confronting the person on the spot is almost inevitably a recipe for disaster. Instead, give yourself time to think it over and to get others' points of view on the matter. Pursue the route that has the greatest potential for mutual understanding and resolution.

Sexual Harassment and Discrimination

A recent survey conducted at a prominent and progressive medical school revealed that over half of all female students felt they had been harassed while in medical school. Many students felt they were frequently treated unfairly.

Each school has protocols for reporting sexual harassment and discrimination based on race, gender, disabilities, religion, and at some schools sexual orientation. If you suspect an abuse of power, in no way should you accept this as the "culture" of medicine. It is up to each of us to transform medical school to be more tolerant and more just. This requires that we call attention to such acts as they occur, to the person involved, and when more serious to the appropriate authorities, or that we file a legal action.

A FRONT-ROW SEAT IN LIFE

Once you manage the basic aspects of survival in medical school, you will appreciate the experiences of these years: studying the anatomy of the pelvis at 3 A.M. before the exam, comforting a young girl after her amputation, or breaking into tears in front of your psychiatry small group. Each experience carries a lesson, one that lectures or this book cannot teach—the mystery of the human body unfolding, the pain and beauty of being close to others, and the knowledge that you gain about yourself.

As a medical school professor once told me, "In medicine, we have a front-row seat in life."

Perhaps the greatest reward is the privilege of being a doctor. Each moment we spend caring for people holds the possibility for profound learning and growth.

APPENDIX A

HOLLAND'S THEORY OF VOCATIONAL PERSONALITIES

In Chapter 1, we discussed career choice from the perspective of the psychologist and career theorist John Holland's theory of personality and work environments. Holland's theory is simple and practical: he believes that individuals seek work environments that allow them to express their personalities.

Holland categorizes personalities and their corresponding work environments into six major types: Realistic, Investigative, Artistic, Social, Enterprising, and Conventional. A person would rarely be one pure type but would have aspects of all six types in varying degrees.

The pattern of a person's three most prevalent types would be her or his subtype. For example, the subtype ISA would describe a person who has investigative, social, and artistic traits, in that order. The following is a brief description of Holland's types.

Realistic individuals are stable, frank, and active. They like athletic or mechanical activities and prefer to work with things (machines, tools, objects, or plants). A typical realistic occupation would be that of mechanic.

Investigative individuals are intellectual and introverted. They like to observe, investigate, analyze, solve complex puzzles, and work analytically with their minds. A typical investigative occupation would be that of biologist.

Artistic individuals are individualistic and expressive. They like to work in unstructured situations using their imagination and creativity. Interior decorating is an example of a typical artistic occupation.

Social individuals are friendly and skilled with words. They like working with people to inform, help, train, develop, or cure them. Career counseling would be a typical social occupation.

Enterprising individuals are extroverted and sociable. They like to work with people to influence, persuade, lead, or manage them for organizational or economic gain. Practicing law is a typical enterprising profession.

Conventional individuals are neat, orderly, and practical. They like to work with data (facts, figures, numbers) in structured settings. They are good at carrying out details or following through on others' instructions. An accountant is an example of a typical conventional-type worker.

APPENDIX B

RESOURCES FOR UNDERSTANDING YOURSELF

For those of you who wish to spend more time understanding yourself, we list a few well-known instruments for assessing vocational interests and values. Your college career center or a private counseling service can give you these tests (or others) and discuss the implications of your test profile for a career in medicine.

INTEREST INVENTORIES

The Self-Directed Search (SDS) is based on John Holland's theory of the relation between personality and career development. A three-digit code, such as I-S-A for a physician, shows a person's first, second, and third highest scores on the SDS. You can take and score this inventory yourself with some direction in about twenty minutes.

The Strong Interest Inventory (SII) can be completed in about thirty minutes and must be scored by machine. Information on the SII is presented as general occupational themes, basic interest scales, and occupational scales. The general occupational themes correspond to Holland's six areas of interest. Each general occupational theme is further divided into two to five basic interest scales, providing more detailed information on patterns of interests. Finally, scores are presented as occupational scales based on the responses of men and women who are employed in their occupations for at least three years and satisfied with their work.

The Vocational Preference Inventory (VPI) is another instrument based on Holland's model. It is used in clinical and counseling settings and provides more information on personality than does the Self-Directed Search (SDS).

VALUES INVENTORIES

The Study of Values by Allport, Vernon, and Lindzey helps you understand your personal values and is useful as a springboard for thinking about what you hold most important in life.

The Values Scale (VS) provides information on twenty-one scales measuring values or satisfactions that people seek in life.

The System of Interactive Guidance and Information (SIGI-Plus) is a computer-based program that assesses and categorizes work values in these ten areas: income, prestige, independence, helping others, security, variety, leadership, leisure, working in one's field of interest, and early entry.

APPENDIX C

SPECIALTY ORGANIZATIONS IN MEDICINE

The medical school phase of a physician's education is called undergraduate medical education. The second phase, graduate medical education, prepares a physician to practice in a specialty. The choice of a specialty area can be daunting for medical students, and competition for certain specialties can be fierce. Most specialty areas provide certification either primarily or as a subspecialty. To obtain additional information, contact one of these specialty academies, boards, or organizations.

AEROSPACE MEDICINE
Aerospace Medical Association
320 S. Henry St.
Alexandria, VA 22314-3579

ALLERGY AND IMMUNOLOGY
American Board of Allergy and Immunology
University City Science Center
3624 Market St.
Philadelphia, PA 19104-2675

ANESTHESIOLOGY
American Board of Anesthesiology
100 Constitution Plaza
Hartford, CT 06103-1796

American Osteopathic College of Anesthesiologists
3511 Bluejacket Dr.
Lee's Summit, MO 64063

CARDIOLOGY
American College of Cardiology
9111 Old Georgetown Rd.
Bethesda, MD 20814

COLON AND RECTAL SURGERY
American Board of Colon and Rectal Surgery
20600 Eureka Rd. #713
Taylor, MI 48180

CRITICAL CARE MEDICINE
Society of Critical Care Medicine
8101 E. Kaiser Ave.
Anaheim, CA 92808

DERMATOLOGY
American Board of Dermatology
Henry Ford Hospital
Detroit, MI 48202

EMERGENCY MEDICINE
American Board of Emergency Medicine
3000 Coolidge Rd.
East Lansing, MI 48823

FAMILY PRACTICE
American Board of Family Practice
2228 Young Dr.
Lexington, KY 40505

GENETICS
American Board of Medical Genetics
9650 Rockville Pike
Bethesda, MD 20814-3998

GERIATRIC MEDICINE
American Geriatrics Society
770 Lexington Ave. #300
New York, NY 10021

HEMATOLOGY
American Society of Hematology
1101 Connecticut Ave. N.W.
Washington, DC 20036

INFECTIOUS DISEASE
Infectious Disease Society of America
201-202 LCI P.O. 3333
New Haven, CT 06510

INTERNAL MEDICINE
American Board of Internal Medicine
3624 Market St.
Philadelphia, PA 19104-2675

American College of Osteopathic Internists
300 Fifth St. N.E.
Washington, DC 20002

American Osteopathic Board of Internal Medicine
5200 S. Ellis Ave.
Chicago, IL 60615

American Society of Internal Medicine
1101 Vermont Ave. N.W. Suite 500
Washington, DC 20005-3457

NEPHROLOGY
American Society of Nephrology
1101 Connecticut Ave. N.W.
Washington, DC 20036

NEUROLOGY
American Association of Neurological Surgeons
22 South Washington St. Suite 100
Park Ridge, IL 60068

American Board of Neurological Surgery
6550 Fanin St. 2139
Houston, TX 77030-2701

American Osteopathic Board of Neurology and Psychiatry
2250 Chapel Ave.
Cherry Hill, NJ 08002

NUCLEAR MEDICINE
American Board of Nuclear Medicine
900 Veteran Ave.
Los Angeles, CA 90024-1786

American College of Nuclear Physicians
1101 Connecticut Ave. N.W. #700
Washington, DC 20036

OBSTETRICS AND GYNECOLOGY
American Board of Obstetrics and Gynecology
936 N. 34th St. #200
Seattle, WA 98103

American College of Obstetricians and Gynecologists
409 12th St. S.W.
Washington, DC 20024

OPHTHALMOLOGY

American Academy of Ophthalmology
655 Beach St.
P.O. Box 7424
San Francisco, CA 94120-7424

American Board of Ophthalmology
111 Presidential Blvd. Suite 241
Bala Cynwyd, PA 19004

American Osteopathic College of Ophthalmology,
Otorhinolaryngology, and Head and Neck Surgery
405 Grand Ave.
Dayton, OH 45405

ORTHOPEDIC SURGERY'

American Academy of Orthopedic Surgeons
222 South Prospect Ave.
Park Ridge, IL 60068

American Board of Orthopedic Surgery
400 Silver Cedar Ct.
Chapel Hill, NC 27514

OTOLARYNGOLOGY

American Academy of Otolaryngology and Head and Neck Surgery
1 Prince St.
Alexandria, VA 22314

American Board of Otolaryngology
5615 Kirby Dr. #936
Houston, TX 77005

PATHOLOGY

American Board of Pathology
Lincoln Center
5401 W. Kennedy Blvd.
P.O. Box 25915
Tampa, FL 33622

PEDIATRICS

American Board of Pediatrics
111 Silver Cedar Ct.
Chapel Hill, NC 27514

PHYSICAL MEDICINE AND REHABILITATION
American Board of Physical Medicine and Rehabilitation
Norwest Center #674
21 First St. S.W.
Rochester, MN 55902

PLASTIC SURGERY
American Board of Plastic Surgery
Seven Penn Center Suite 400
1635 Market St.
Philadelphia, PA 19103-2204

American Society of Plastic and Reconstructive Surgeons
444 East Algonquin Rd.
Arlington Heights, IL 60005

PREVENTIVE MEDICINE
American Board of Preventive Medicine
9950 W. Lawrence Ave. Suite 106
Schiller Park, IL 60176

American College of Preventive Medicine
1015 15th St. N.W. #403
Washington, DC 20005

American Osteopathic College of Preventive Medicine
1900 The Exchange #160
Atlanta, GA 30339-2022

PSYCHIATRY AND NEUROLOGY
American Board of Psychiatry and Neurology
500 Lake Cook Rd. Suite 335
Deerfield, IL 60015

American Psychiatric Association
1400 K St. N.W.
Washington, DC 20005

RADIOLOGY
American Board of Radiology
5255 E. Williams Circle Suite 6800
Tucson, AZ 85711

American College of Radiology
1891 Preston White Dr.
Reston, VA 22091

American Osteopathic College of Radiology
119 E. Second St.
Milan, MO 63556

RHEUMATOLOGY
American College of Rheumatology
60 Executive Park South #150
Atlanta, GA 30329

SURGERY
American Board of Surgery
1617 John F. Kennedy Blvd. Suite 860
Philadelphia, PA 19103-1847

American College of Osteopathic Surgeons
123 Henry St.
Alexandria, VA 22314

American College of Surgeons
55 E. Erie St.
Chicago, IL 60611

THORACIC SURGERY
American Board of Thoracic Surgery
One Rotary Center Suite 803
Evanston, IL 60201

American Thoracic Society
1740 Broadway
New York, NY 10019

Society of Thoracic Surgeons
111 East Wacker Dr. Suite 600
Chicago, IL 60601

UROLOGY
American Board of Urology
31700 Telegraph Rd. Suite 150
Bingham Farms, MI 48025

American Urological Association
Office of Education
6750 West Loop South Suite 900
Bellaire, TX 77401-4114

APPENDIX D
MEDICAL ORGANIZATIONS

Accreditation Council for Continuing Medical Education
515 N. State St. Suite 7340
Chicago, IL 60610-4377
(312) 464-2500

American Association of Colleges of Osteopathic Medicine
6110 Executive Blvd. Suite 405
Rockville, MD 20852
(301) 468-0990

American Medical Association
Department of Undergraduate Medical Education
515 N. State St.
Chicago, IL 60610
(312) 464-5000, Ext. 4691

American Medical Students Association
1902 Association Dr.
Reston, VA 20191
(703) 620-6600

American Osteopathic Association
142 E. Ontario
Chicago, IL 60611
(312) 280-5800

Association of American Medical Colleges
2450 N St. N.W.
Washington, DC 20037
(202) 828-0400

National Board of Osteopathic Medical Examiners
2700 River Rd. Suite 407
Des Plaines, IL 60018
(847) 635-9955

National Medical Association
1012 Tenth St. N.W.
Washington, DC 20001
(202) 347-1895

ON-LINE INFORMATION ABOUT MEDICINE

The Internet provides up-to-date information on medical issues and practice. A guide to the Internet for physicians is now available (see References for Chapter 2). In addition, Web pages for medical organizations and schools are growing in number and offer a good source of information. On-line discussion groups also can help you get an inside perspective.

What is available on the Internet changes rapidly. Here is a sample of what is available.

WORLD WIDE WEB

American Medical Association
http://www.ama-assn.org

Journal of Family Practice
http://www.phymac.med.wayne.edu/jfp/jfp.htm

Managed Care Glossary
http://www.bcm.tmc.edu/ama-mss/glossary.html

Med Access
Posts information that the health care community provides voluntarily.
http://www.medacfcces.com

E-MAIL AND LISTSERVS

American Medical News
amedltr@aol.com
General questions.

Mhcare-L
Subscribe listserv@mizzou1.missouri.edu
Managed health care, quality.

Subscribe listserv@utmb.edu
Mutual support group for residents.

NEWSGROUPS

Use your newsreader to scan topics such as sci.med,
sci.med.diseases.cancer, sci.med.telemedicine, and sci.med.vision.

GOPHER SITES

Gopher provides access to a variety of related databases at a single
site.

Medical List
gopher una.hh.lib.umich.edu

MedSearch
gopher gopher.medsearch.com

National Library of Medicine
gopher gopher.nlm.nih.gov

Ruralnet
gopher ruralnet.mu.wvnet.edu

REFERENCES AND SUGGESTED READINGS

GENERAL INFORMATION

Zipperer, L., ed. 1995. *The Health Care Almanac: A Resource Guide to the Medical Field*. Chicago: American Medical Association.

CHAPTER 1

Dossey, L. 1991. *Meaning and Medicine*. New York: Bantam.

Reynolds, R., and J. Stone, eds. 1991. *On Doctoring*. New York: Simon & Schuster.

CHAPTER 2

Bodenheimer, T. S., and K. Grumbach. 1995. *Understanding Health Policy: A Clinical Approach*. Norwalk, Conn.: Appleton & Lange.

Eikleberry, C. 1995. *The Career Guide for Creative and Unconventional People*. Berkeley, Calif.: Ten Speed Press.

Ferguson, T. 1996. *Health Online*. Reading, Mass.: Addison-Wesley.

The Future of Medical Practice. Chicago: American Medical Association, Council on Long-Range Planning and Development.

Hancock, L. 1995. *The Physician's Guide to the Internet*. Issaquah, Wash.: Lippincott-Raven.

Heuston, M. C. 1996. *The Doctor's Directory of Medical Internet Addresses*. Scottsdale, Ariz.: Value Network.

Hogarth, M., and D. Hutchinson. n.d. *An Internet Guide for the Health Professional*. http://www.midtown.net/formation to download the first edition free.

Larson, P. F., M. Osterweis, and E. Rubin, eds. 1994. *Health Workforce Issues in the 21st Century*. Washington, D.C.: Association of Academic Health Centers.

Linden, T., and M. Kienholz. 1995. *Dr. Tom Linden's Guide to Online Medicine*. New York: McGraw-Hill.

Ramsdell, M., ed. 1994. *My First Year as a Doctor*. New York: Walker.

Trends in U.S. Health Care. 1995. Chicago: American Medical Association.

CHAPTER 3

Iserson, K. 1993. *Getting into a Residency: A Guide for Medical Students*. 3d ed. Tucson, Ariz.: Galen Press.

Opportunities: The Directory of Osteopathic Post-Doctoral Education Programs, 1995–1996. Chicago: American Osteopathic Association/American Osteopathic Health Care Association.

Rucker, D. T., and M. D. Keller, eds. 1990. *Careers in Medicine: Traditional and Alternative Opportunities*. Rev. ed. Garrett Park, Md.: Garrett Park Press.

Swartz, H. M., and D. L. Gottheil. 1993. *The Education of Physician-Scholars: Preparing for Leadership in the Health Care System*. Rockville, Md.: Betz Publishing.

CHAPTER 4

Holliman, C. J., ed. 1995. *Resident's Guide to Starting in Medical Practice*. Baltimore: Williams & Wilkins.

CHAPTER 5

Pope, L. 1995. *Looking Beyond the Ivy League: Finding the College That's Right for You*. Rev. ed. New York: Penguin.

Wilson, E. 1993. *The 100 Best Colleges for African-American Students*. New York: Penguin.

CHAPTER 7

Casewit, C. 1994. *Summer Adventures*. New York: Macmillan.

Clouser, K. D. 1990. Humanities in Medical Education: Some Contributions. *Journal of Medicine and Philosophy* 15:289–301.

Covey, S. 1995. *First Things First*. New York: Simon & Schuster.

Olson, A. 1994. *Alternatives to the Peace Corps: A Directory of Third World and U.S. Volunteer Opportunities*. Oakland, Calif.: Food First Books.

CHAPTER 9

Hassan, A., ed. 1994. *A Complete Preparation for the MCAT*. 6th ed. Rockville, Md.: Betz Publishing.

The MCAT Practice Test II and Sample Items. 1993. Washington, D.C.: Association of American Medical Colleges.

The MCAT Practice Test III. 1993. Washington, D.C.: Association of American Medical Colleges.

The MCAT Student Manual. 1993. Washington, D.C.: Association of American Medical Colleges.

Rudman, J. 1995. *The New Rudman's Questions and Answers on the MCAT*. Syosset, N.Y.: National Learning Corp.

CHAPTER 10

Education of the Osteopathic Physician. 1990. Rockville, Md.: American Association of Colleges of Osteopathic Medicine.

Graduate Medical Education Directory, 1995–1996. Chicago: American Medical Association.

Minority Student Opportunities in U.S. Medical Schools. Washington, D.C.: Association of American Medical Colleges.

CHAPTER 11

Covey, S. 1989. *The Seven Habits of Highly Effective People*. New York: Simon & Schuster.

Medical School Admission Requirements. Updated yearly. Washington, D.C.: Association of American Medical Colleges.

Osteopathic Medical College Information. 1997 Entering Class. Updated yearly. Rockville, Md.: American Association of Colleges of Osteopathic Medicine.

CHAPTER 13

Hendrie, H. C., and C. Lloyd, eds. 1990. *Educating Competent and Humane Physicians*. Bloomington: Indiana University Press.

INDEX

ABOUT THE AUTHORS

Jennifer Danek is a student at the University of California School of Medicine, San Francisco. After two years as a chemistry major at James Madison University in Virginia, she transferred to the University of California, San Diego, where she majored in chemistry and then Third World studies. As an undergraduate, she was active with student cooperatives, the women's collective, and alternative media. She spent the year before medical school working with a women's health center and plant medicine project in rural Nicaragua.

Jennifer worked on this book between her senior year in college and her third year of medical school. In that time, she taught incarcerated youth in San Francisco Youth Guidance Center and worked with area high schools and community health projects. In her free time, she enjoys Brazilian and Middle Eastern dance, creative writing, and cooking. Her goals are to improve the quality of life and opportunities for youth, to contribute to international health, and to learn about the various traditions of healing. In 1996 she received the Chancellor's Award for Public Service and the Thomas N. Burbridge Award from UCSF.

Marita Danek is a professor in the Department of Counseling at Gallaudet University, Washington, D.C., and Director of the Rehabilitation Counseling Program. She received a Ph.D. degree in counseling from the University of Maryland, College Park, in 1979. She has worked in the counseling field for almost three decades as a rehabilitation counselor, school counselor, and counselor educator. Marita has published extensively in the counseling literature and has received numerous professional awards, including the Research in Counseling Award from the American Counseling Association. In 1994 she spent her sabbatical as a Visiting Fellow at Massey University in Palmerston North, New Zealand. Her interests include travel and hybridizing daylilies.